W9-AZG-468

PRAISE FOR *WHY THE PRINCIPALSHIP?*

"The attention this book gives to the civilities of leadership—public speaking, listening, and going on television—is worth the price of the book, and we will add this to our media instruction at The Buckley School of Public Speaking." —**Reid Buckley**, best-selling author of numerous books, including *An American Family: The Buckleys*

"I am a little more than halfway through my master's program and find this a must-read book. It speaks to me as if a travel agent is mapping my graduate school adventure to ensure success. I like the quotes that introduce each chapter and the references to research and writing that I can use in assigned papers. The 'snapshots' are stories that tell me what I should and should not do to successfully complete my master's degree." —**Joseph Ellinger**, full-time graduate student, Georgia State University

"Dale L. Brubaker and Misti Williams have written a very practical guide that will help the aspiring administrator move smoothly into the role of school leader. The header quotes that introduce and guide the chapters are especially meaningful, and the questions for discussion at the end of each chapter will aid professional development communities as administrative interns, mentors, and school leaders come together to talk about what is best for students and teachers." —**Vicky Ratchford**, professor, School of Education, Gardner-Webb University

Why the Principalship?

Making the Leap from the Classroom

DALE L. BRUBAKER AND MISTI WILLIAMS

ROWMAN & LITTLEFIELD EDUCATION

A Division of
ROWMAN & LITTLEFIELD PUBLISHERS, INC.
Lanham • New York • Toronto • Plymouth, UK

Published by Rowman & Littlefield Education
A division of Rowman & Littlefield Publishers, Inc.
A wholly owned subsidiary of The Rowman & Littlefield Publishing Group, Inc.
4501 Forbes Boulevard, Suite 200, Lanham, Maryland 20706
http://www.rowmaneducation.com

Estover Road, Plymouth PL6 7PY, United Kingdom

British Library Cataloguing in Publication Information Available

Library of Congress Cataloging-in-Publication Data

Brubaker, Dale L.
  Why the principalship? : making the leap from the classroom / Dale L. Brubaker and Misti Williams.
    p. cm.
  Includes bibliographical references and index.
  ISBN 978-1-60709-771-6 (cloth : alk. paper)—ISBN 978-1-60709-772-3 (pbk. : alk. paper)— ISBN 978-1-60709-773-0 (electronic)
  1. School principals—Training of—United States. 2. School principals—Vocational guidance—United States. 3. School administrators—Vocational guidance—United States. 4. Educational leadership—United States. I. Williams, Misti. II. Title.
LB2831.92.B8 2010
371.2'012023—dc22   2010011253

∞ ™ The paper used in this publication meets the minimum requirements of American National Standard for Information Sciences—Permanence of Paper for Printed Library Materials, ANSI/NISO Z39.48-1992.

Printed in the United States of America

For our students—
past, present, and future

Contents

Preface

The first two questions most book readers ask are, "Who is this book written for?" and "How will it speak to me?" The primary audience for this book is teachers and others who want to be credentialed as school administrators.

In order to speak to you with a clear and understandable voice, we will address you throughout the book in the second person. Our aim in doing so is to stimulate thought and discussion among you, fellow candidates for principal certification, university professors of educational administration, school administrators interested in helping you as mentors, intern advisors, and central office administrators with a stake in your success.

These members of your support group should find this book useful in guiding you through your preparation program. The appendixes at the end of the book provide materials that preservice and in-service leaders can use for educational administration courses, leadership seminars, and other related activities. References to appropriate appendixes at the end of the book will be made throughout the book. There are also suggested readings at the end of each chapter.

Our interest as authors, researchers, and professors of educational leadership is in the transitional career stage from teacher to school administrator. The results of this interest are documented in books, articles, and monographs written at the University of North Carolina at Greensboro (Brubaker, 2004, 2006; Brubaker & Coble, 2005, 2007a, 2007b; and Williams, 2009).

The present book extends our previous research and writing. Our special interest has been in the role of professional development for teacher leaders, assistant principals, principals, superintendents, and other central office leaders.

This interest in professional development is based on the premise that our investment in people now will pay off many times over in the future. "The three largest expenditures of funds in this country" are "health expenditures . . . , the U.S. Department of Defense . . . , and elementary and secondary education" (Gallagher, 2007, p. 27). The preparation of candidates for positions of school leadership is obviously an important element of our investment in schools and schooling.

The first thing to note as a student in a preparation program for the principalship is the variety of programs that exist, one of which you are or will soon be a participant in. Traditional programs, usually in universities, have courses such as educational finance, educational theory, and school law, followed by some kind of field experience.

Lynn Olson (2007, p. 53) believes that this "scattershot approach increasingly is giving way to dramatically different forms of principal preparation." In particular, there is a shift to greater emphasis on curriculum, instruction, and student achievement. Research and writing on school leadership is also emphasized more, with less attention given to managerial skills.

Lynn Olson notes several important aspects of some new preparation programs in her critique of changes in recent years: more rigorous selection and recruitment of candidates and a more coherent curriculum "deeply rooted in practice, focused on the principal's role in improving instruction and student achievement, and designed to ensure mastery of core competencies by engaging participants in solving real-world problems through case studies, school-based projects, and simulations" (2007, p. 54). She also mentions opportunities to practice school leadership early in preparatory programs and new roles for school districts as partners and other nonprofit providers.

We urge you as readers to update yourselves on different preparation programs through reviews of the literature and conferences where attendees from programs other than your own will share what they have learned and their assessments of such programs. Professional development habits developed during your administrator preparation program should carry over into the assistant principalship. We must also add that online courses continue to play a greater role in universities in general and preparation programs in particular.

The point we wish to make is that the present book gives attention to steps most, if not all, candidates will experience in working toward principal certification. We will walk you through these steps. Chapter 1, "Introduction: 'A Leap of Faith,'" speaks to your decision to enter a preparation program. The case for a proactive stance on your part is made and prospects and pitfalls during a preparation program are discussed. Being clear as to your purpose for entering a preparation program will serve you well as you move forward. We refer to this as your *personal vision.*

In chapter 1, as well as those that follow, we will present snapshots—brief sketches—that illustrate key points. Issues are important, but how people are affected by them comes to life when a personal face is placed on the issues. Snapshots tell stories that take you, the reader, backstage into the lives of preparation program participants we have known. Some of these snapshots are descriptions of what we have experienced in our own lives. Others are composites of candidates we have related to as graduate student mentors and professors.

What is it about this book that is unique? It affords the reader the opportunity to get behind the eyes of educators trying to place their administrative careers on track.

Chapter 2, "Now What? Leaving Teaching on a High Note: 'One Foot In and One Foot Out,'" describes lessons learned in teaching that can be helpful in preparation program activities, such as courses, observations in schools, and other field-related experiences.

Chapter 3, "Composing a Meaningful Personal Curriculum while Taking Educational Administration Courses," rests on the assumption that an administrator preparation curriculum is more than a course of study. It includes the highly personal hidden curriculum and unintended learning a candidate may experience.

Chapter 4, "Negotiating a Successful Internship," urges you, the reader and preparation candidate, to actively construct meaningful field-experience frameworks for learning and a network of personal contacts. It is during this phase of the preparation program that you are most likely to acquire one or more mentors. These mentors may be important in "Seeking a Position as an

Assistant Principal," the title of chapter 5. The interviewing process is one of several subjects in this chapter that focus on your presentation of self.

Chapter 6, "First Days on the Job as an Assistant Principal," takes you through many of the details and challenges you will face as you begin your administrative career. The reality of life on "the firing line" comes to life in this chapter. We focus in chapter 6 on the assistant principalship because most administrators make their way to principalships and central office positions by way of the assistant principalship.

It should be noted that there are those who criticize states for giving salary increases to teachers who take courses in administration and leadership even though they may never become assistant principals and/or principals. At the same time, it may be argued that teacher leadership in schools is increasingly important and leadership courses taken by those who may never become assistant principals and/or principals can make a positive difference in a school's culture.

You will note that header quotes introduce each chapter, thus setting the tone for the writing that follows. You may want to return to these quotes as you make your way through each chapter, as they are reminders of the feeling established by us as authors.

At the end of each chapter there is a set of questions for discussion or use in a "professional learning community" of future school leaders and their mentors. Suggested readings are also in this section of each chapter.

Ideas throughout the book are anchored in important research and writing conducted by scholars interested in schools and educational leadership. References to their books and articles are cited using American Psychological Association (APA) format.

Many of you will find the appendixes at the end of the book personally useful as you read this book, while others will use these materials in a professional development leadership role. Professional development opportunities for school-system central office leaders, school administrators, and higher education consultants to school systems may be realized by using the appendixes in a variety of settings.

A major thesis in this book is that professional development leaders learn as much from their followers as their followers learn from them. We therefore encourage teacher leaders working on school administration certification to avail themselves of as many professional development opportunities as they can both as leaders and as followers. There are, throughout this book, examples of how this can be accomplished. Many of these examples are in snapshots.

References and an index conclude the book. In the conversational spirit of this book we urge you to write us at our e-mail addresses so that we can converse with each other: dlbrubak@uncg.edu and mwsoutha@uncg.edu. We promise a response.

Acknowledgments

Our special appreciation and thanks go to graduate students who shared stories about what they experienced when going through principal preparation programs. Joseph Ellinger getting on track in his master's program at Georgia State University was the original impetus for writing this book. The details of his story, as shared by him, his mother, and his sister, were inspirational, for they made clear how a master's program can be a transformational marker event in a person's life. His story reminds us of the important role universities can play in the lives of their students, something we too often take for granted.

We also want to acknowledge the research and writing of Seymour B. Sarason, friend and professor emeritus of psychology at Yale University, and his seminal work on the creation of educational settings and school culture. Sarason writes about the importance of being hopeful, if not optimistic, in writing about schools and schooling, something we kept in mind in writing this book. We were pleased when he found *Why the Principalship? Making the Leap from the Classroom* to be such a book (Sarason, 2009).

Rebecca Starnes, from Greensboro's family council, brought our attention to ways to frame the role of stress in leaders' lives in a stimulating lecture at a Sunday night forum. Thank you, Rebecca, for your contribution to the last chapter in our book.

All authors know the importance of excellent editors and production staff. It does indeed take a community to give birth to a book. We especially want to thank Thomas F. Koerner, vice president and editorial director, Rowman & Littlefield Education. His experience in school administration and higher education placed him in a unique position to make suggested changes that strengthened the book. He and Maera Stratton, assistant editor, acquisitions, showed us every courtesy authors could want.

Imagining Myself as a School Administrator

Applying to a Principal Preparation Program

Taking Courses

Internship

Applying/Interviewing for an Assistant Principalship

First Days as an Assistant Principal

First Steps in Becoming a School Administrator

1

Introduction: "A Leap of Faith"

The voluntary taking of serious chances is a means for the maintenance and acquisition of character.

—*Erving Goffman (1967, p. 238)*

We owe everything to human creativity. Everything that lasts, that changes our lives, that emerges from what was once unimaginable has its roots in that initial spark of innovation.

—*Joshua Cooper Ramo (2009, p. 240)*

Often you will hear them say, "I never expected to wind up here." Maybe that's the secret to leadership.

—*Anna Quindlen (2005, p. 86)*

So you want to be a school administrator! You want to leave classroom teaching and be responsible for all of the students in the school and all of the adults in the school, especially teachers! Have you really thought through what this will mean in your professional life and in your life outside of school as well? In this chapter we will engage you in a conversation that introduces you to the transition from teacher to school administrator.

NEW BEGINNINGS AND REALITIES

The first reality to note is that any transition, including the one from teacher to school administrator, involves a sense of loss and a sense of adventure. You will be moving from a position of stability in which you have learned to be comfortable and successful into a transitional structure.

One master's in school administration (MSA) student described this transition period as "one foot in and one foot out." This graphically describes the challenge of keeping one's balance in such a challenging time in one's career and life. (See appendix D, "Dealing with Contradictions in Principal Preparation Programs and Beyond.")

Termination from an existing professional and life structure can be painful and full of contradictions. A number of questions will naturally emerge: Will my teacher colleagues and friends accept me for who I am and what I will be expected to do in my transition toward a new administrative role? How will my students react to my transition? How will parents view me as I move toward a new administrative role? What will the promises and pitfalls be in my school administrator preparation program?

Will I be able to embrace separate and contradictory "truths" that face me in the transition toward the role of school administrator? For example, will I be able to enjoy the sense of adventure while at the same time being told that I must uphold some questionable school policies and traditions associated with the structure of the school? Will I be willing and able to return to teaching if school administration is not for me?

SNAPSHOT 1.1: A NEW BEGINNING

When I began to think about applying for the MSA program I had some apprehension, but I knew it was time to take on a new challenge. I enjoyed teaching, but I had begun to lose the sizzle that I felt when I entered the profession. I told a friend that I was getting tired of hearing myself teach much of the same old material.

I was excited and happy to get my acceptance to the program in the mail. One of my first thoughts was that I would be leaving the narrow focus of the classroom and have more life space as a school administrator. I was also somewhat anxious, as I knew that as an administrator I would be challenged to form new allegiances and alliances and I would be standing in the gap at times supporting teachers, not administrators.

I would also have to represent the administrative point of view at other times, something that would bring me in conflict with my former teaching colleagues. This thought made me realize for the first time that I would reflect at times as an administrator on why I had left teaching and the classroom for this new larger world of conflict and responsibility. (See appendix E, "The Joy of Teaching and Leading.")

I knew that I was at the time and place where I needed to show proof of some leadership I had shown and have a platform statement of beliefs or philosophy that would demonstrate that I was ready to enter a principal preparation program. There was work for me to do to get ready for the next step.

We often think about three stages students experience in a principal preparation program: getting started, maintaining the momentum in the day-to-day activities of coursework and the internship, and completing degree requirements. You are expected to be a starter, maintainer, and closer.

Some students, like the one in the previous snapshot, have a mix of feelings about a new start-up. They are somewhat discontented with the present and feel anxious about leaving its comfort while being stimulated in anticipating a new adventure. Some students say they have a particularly difficult time grinding it out during the maintenance stage. And still others find it hard to finish the degree.

The challenge is to be honest with yourself as to strengths and weaknesses you have had in each stage while being involved in previous degree programs, after which you will find ways to continue pushing on when you have a tendency to get stuck in a particular stage.

It is natural that you will at times experience a crisis in confidence. You will need to remind yourself of victories, large and small, that you have experienced in your journey toward the completion of your educational leadership program. Success breeds confidence in your ability to do good work. This confidence in turn breeds more success. Momentum toward reaching your vision of becoming a school administrator is the key to getting on track and staying on track. (See appendix A, "Selecting a School Principal Licensure Program.")

Idealism often plays a role in a new start-up for you, the prospective school administrator. Memories of good principals and assistant principals can be inspirational and motivating. You may have experienced such leaders as a K–12 student and/or a teacher. They serve as beacons of hope, and you will probably want to try to do many of the things they did so well. The following snapshot illustrates how a principal planted a seed of hope that was later nourished by a professor of educational administration.

SNAPSHOT 1.2: ONE PLUS ONE EQUALS TWO POSITIVE SOURCES OF SUPPORT

When I began teaching I had a principal I considered an excellent leader. He was kind but firm and always found a positive way to convey even the most negative information. His impact on my realization that I wanted to become a school leader could have been some form of "hero worship." I not only wanted to be like him, but I also wanted him to be proud of me. I associated with a school leader for the first time ever. I began to think like a principal and to evaluate issues that occurred in our school from a larger perspective. It was scary and comfortable all at the same time. My intuitive perception of school leadership began.

What happened next was in the MSA program and it was unre-markable. The simplicity of it could have escaped me but instead made a profound impact on my academic career. My professor at that time was superb. He could illuminate the most complicated idea, making you feel that you understood it all along.

He often told us that we served a "board of directors" in our minds, a group of people that we thought of when we made important decisions. We might think, "What would my grand-mother (or whoever) think of me?" His assignment was to write a paper describing our board and why we believed each person was a part of our board. I will never forget what was written on the last page: "Stellar comments. You have what it takes." The epiphany strikes again! I believed in that instant that I could and importantly should continue my degree. (See appendix H, "Traits of Outstanding Leaders.")

You may also remember poorly performing assistant principals and principals and not want to repeat their mistakes. There may be times during your edu-cational leadership program, particularly the internship, when the faces and actions of these administrators seem to be etched in your mind as you say to yourself that you don't want to behave as these poor administrators did. You don't want students and teachers to suffer from such experiences.

A second reality during the transitional period from teacher to school administrator is how demanding it can be on your resources of time, energy, and money. Like teaching, being a first-rate student in a principal preparation program is hard work.

Many students begin work on their degree while teaching. Evenings, week-ends, and summers are filled with class assignments, time in higher education classrooms, online work, and internships. Financial issues can force you and perhaps your family to tighten your belts in order to pay for tuition, books, and travel. Student loans can mount up, thus putting more financial pressure on you and those you love.

Some of you are full-time fellows with stipends, but such outside help is usually less than you would earn as a full-time teacher. In short, sacrifices and suspended gratification, such as postponed vacations and the like, are called for in order to complete your credentialing for a school administration position. Hopefully you will feel this is worth it, but there will be times when you may wonder if this is the case. (See appendix G, "A Personal Leadership Change and Conservation Inventory.") The following snapshot speaks to this challenge.

SNAPSHOT 1.3: A STUDENT STRUGGLES WITH FINANCIAL PRESSURES

It was a beautiful spring day when I headed for my Cases and Concepts in Educational Administration class at the university. I arrived at the four-story parking lot and noticed that one of my newly purchased tires was nearly flat. There was a cut in the tire, probably from a curb that I hit, that couldn't be repaired. And I hadn't purchased the additional warranty when I bought the tires.

My mind began working overtime as to how I was going to pay for a new tire as well as several other bills that had accumulated that month. I had already borrowed money for tuition, and books for the semester were more than two hundred dollars. It was the convergence of these problems that depressed me as I walked from the parking lot to my university classroom.

Fortunately, when I settled into my class for the evening I realized that I had a community of support in my fellow students and professors, who cared about me professionally and personally. I recognized the power of gratitude as a source of inspiration to continue my work in the program.

Time and energy normally devoted to family and friends frequently give way to university requirements for educational leadership programs. The following snapshot takes us backstage as a degree candidate describes how telling this pressure can be.

SNAPSHOT 1.4: WHAT ABOUT ME?
AND OTHER DIFFICULT QUERIES
FROM LOVED ONES

I distinctly remember leaving work to pick up my four-year-old at day care. She had come down with something and my husband, who worked only two minutes away, could not retrieve her.

I drove into the parking lot and let my mind race, making plans for how to balance her care and the two classes I had that evening. I almost had it figured out when the director met me at the door and asked for picture identification. I had never picked my daughter up and the day care workers did not recognize me. My plans for how to get to class dissolved, and I cried all the way home. What had I sacrificed to get this degree? That particular question in many forms would haunt me over and over again.

I learned how important faith in my original decision to pursue the MSA was, how essential it was to sometimes deal with financial hardship, and how to do my best to achieve a balance between MSA requirements and family issues. Most of all, I discovered I could live with dilemmas to be reconciled rather than problems to be solved. Not only were there few easy answers, but there were frequently challenges with no apparent answers at the moment. Once again, faith in my vision to complete the program got me through each day.

A third reality of the transitional period from teacher to credentialed school administrator is the sense of loneliness you will sometimes feel and the need for a new small group of friends and colleagues. You are in the process of leaving a few teaching colleagues who have become close friends.

A core group of fellow students may be very helpful to you as you take on the challenges during the transitional period. These are people with whom you can share intimacies and relax backstage. You can share predictable problems that will arise as you make your way through the program: "What might go wrong or did go wrong and what can we do about it?" The sharing of different perspectives will help you avoid too narrow a view of problems, and you will celebrate individual and group victories that will inspire you to continue to do good work in the program.

Conversations with students make it clear that their friends provide both intellectual and social support throughout the program. Students often proofread papers for each other and share information about how to negotiate program requirements. Emotional support is also shared when friends get down on themselves concerning problems that surface. Some of these problems are program-related, whereas others are located in the schools where candidates teach and lead.

Some educational leadership programs encourage and support students going to conferences and conventions that focus on school leadership. These events introduce students to a variety of new ideas and afford the opportunity to build professional networks that may still be in place when students become school administrators. One student described major learning acquired at a conference session that became the topic for discussion in a Cases and Concepts in Educational Leadership class at the university.

SNAPSHOT 1.5: PRIVILEGE AS A SOURCE OF POWER FOR GRADUATE STUDENTS

One of the best sessions I attended at the conference was on sources of power. There was a panel discussion involving two professors, who served as advisors, and two students. Panel members were from four different universities. Gender and ethnic differences were represented on the panel. I was surprised at how informal and candid panel members were during their brief presentations and discussion.

A male student on the panel said that he was one of the few men in a cohort of fifteen students. He noticed on many occasions, particularly in small breakout groups in class, that women deferred to him during discussions and also asked him to be their spokesperson who reported to the larger class. He said that at first he didn't know what to do about this and discussed this with his male advisor, a professor in the program and chair of the educational administration department.

His advisor responded as follows: "Don't worry about it. Privilege takes many forms and you may as well use whatever forms are available to you. In fact, in my position as department chair I use male privilege as a source of power to get things for our department." This triggered a firestorm of reactions from other panel members and the audience of approximately fifty people at the conference.

It was clear to me that the issue of privilege was one that I needed to address in my life as a graduate student and school administrator who will give leadership not only in the school but also in the school system itself. (See appendix O, "Sources of Power Available to You as an Educational Leader and Decision Maker," and appendix B, "The 'Table Manners' of Graduate Student Leadership in a Principal Preparation Program.")

In conclusion, this chapter helps us see that emotional support for you and your friends in the graduate program is essential to your success. This family of friends is obvious to us as professors of educational administration at graduation time. Groups of graduating students socialize, often with their parents and other family members, to celebrate the students' successful completion of the program. This provides us with the opportunity to hear humorous stories about what students experienced in class and out of class. It gives us a chance to have a more encompassing view of the program.

Malcolm Gladwell, author of the bestselling *Outliers: The Story of Success,* summarizes the connection between social savvy and family: "Social savvy is *knowledge.* It's a set of skills that have to be learned. It has to come from somewhere, and the place where we seem to get these kinds of attitudes and skills is from our families" (2008, p. 102).

In the next chapter we will give attention to how your experiences as a teacher and teacher leader can be helpful to you during the transitional period from teacher to school administrator.

QUESTIONS FOR DISCUSSION

1. What prompted you to apply for the principal certification program? Please try to place your reasons in priority order. If you are already in the program, has your list of reasons changed in any way? Your priority order of reasons?
2. Were there any obstacles you anticipated in getting into the principal certification program? Did you experience these obstacles during the application process? Were there any unanticipated obstacles that you experienced? If so, how powerful were they, and how did you overcome them?
3. Who were the key people who supported your application to and entrance into the principal certification program? What role did they play and what was your reaction to their support?
4. What advice would you give to educators who are considering applying to principal certification programs? Please be as specific as possible.
5. How do the epigraphs at the beginning of the chapter speak to you at this point in your first steps in becoming a school administrator?

SUGGESTED READINGS

Brubaker, D. L. (2006). *The charismatic leader: The presentation of self and the creation of educational settings.* Thousand Oaks, CA: Corwin Press. See chapter 2, "Teams, teaming, and the creation of educational settings."

Brubaker, D. L., & Coble, L. D. (2007a). *Staying on track: An educational leader's guide to preventing derailment and ensuring personal and organizational success.*

Thousand Oaks, CA: Corwin Press. See chapter 7, "The seasons of an educational leader's career," those seasons being "Preparing the Way to Become an Educational Administrator," "Entering Educational Administration," "Settling In—the Middle Years," and "The Later Years as an Educational Administrator."

Brubaker, D. L., & Coble, L. D. (2007b). *Teacher renewal: Stories of inspiration to balance your life.* Clemmons, NC: On Track Press.

Darling-Hammond, L. (2007, January 10). A Marshall Plan for teaching: What it will take to leave No Child Left Behind. *Education Week, 48,* 28.

Gladwell, M. (2008). *Outliers: The story of success.* New York: Little, Brown & Co.

McCourt, F. (2005). *Teacher man.* New York: Scribner.

2

Now What? Leaving Teaching on a High Note: "One Foot In and One Foot Out"

The great teachers fill you up with hope and shower you with a thousand reasons to embrace all aspects of life.

—*Pat Conroy (2002, p. 63)*

I've learned that people will forget what you said, people will forget what you did, but people will never forget how you made them feel.

—*Maya Angelou (December 2009, p. 27)*

Once you've left a position and try to return you don't quite click anymore.

—*Chris Matthews (2008)*

Taking the first step is definitely the most difficult in any new endeavor. It means that if you go forward you go to something unknown and if you retreat you think you have failed. It is a moment of commitment and courage we should tuck away for those times when we are dealing with an angry parent or coaxing a fourth grader from underneath the bus. When asked, can we say what compelled us to take the leap of faith? To leave what is familiar and comfortable for something completely foreign? (See appendix G, "A Personal Leadership Change and Conservation Inventory.")

SNAPSHOT 2.1: WHAT WAS I THINKING?

After only three years as a principal, when people ask why I decided to be an administrator, the answer does not roll off my tongue. I have to stop and think about the catalyst for all this. After all, I was a great teacher. My dad was a teacher. My husband was a teacher. I loved teaching. My husband and I used to look at each other and say, "Can you believe they pay us to do this?" Why would I give this up to be an administrator? Is the epiphany so fleeting? I generally say that I left the classroom to make a greater impact on the classroom, but what does that mean?

What in the world compelled me, with two children and a husband, to attend graduate school as many as three nights a week in a town forty-five minutes away? What passion kept me going? I must have known then, but now it is not so clear. When people say, "How did you do it?" I respond that I have a saint for a husband and that I am driven.

Is that all? Certainly there must have been a deeper, more powerful feeling involved at the time. Why can't I recapture it now and put it into words for aspiring principals? I think there was a time when the passion was evident. It's that passion that helped me leave a classroom so familiar for a very unfamiliar journey. (See appendix E, "The Joy of Teaching and Leading.")

SUSTAINING THE PASSION

Passion may be evident at the beginning of our journey into leadership, but what sustains this passion, makes us stay for the long haul? We may ask ourselves this as we feel that we are leaping from a tall building, about to take the next step, really graduate. It's almost as if students never really expect it to happen.

Classes are fine. It actually enhances our teaching or current roles to meet and share with colleagues, read, and write, but then what? Many students teach or maintain their current roles while completing graduate school. This gives the illusion that things won't actually change. Perhaps they can just stay put.

SNAPSHOT 2.2: THE BEST TEACHING YEAR EVER

The last year of graduate school was like a long-awaited haircut. You set the appointment, wait for months, and suffer through many bad hair days. Then on the day of the appointment, your hair falls perfectly into place. It never looked better! You even consider canceling the appointment and just keeping the style you have. Well, the last year of my master's degree studies, I had the best teaching year ever. I had wonderful students, a great principal, and a super schedule. I began to think that I might just keep the style I had!

I began to question whether or not the principalship was what I really wanted. I critically looked at what my current principal and assistant principals had to do each day and wondered if it was really for me. I took a more and more negative perspective on the administrative role as graduation drew near. The licensure exam brought even more trepidation, and I wondered why I was doing this to myself. I loved teaching! I did not have to change.

There it is. The dirty word, "change." For forty-two credit hours and a couple of hectic years, you can almost forget that you are about to undergo a change not only in jobs but also in perspectives. Maybe it's so gradual that you don't even realize that you are beginning to criticize the principal and the decisions he makes. Maybe it sneaks up on you that you now look at your school with a larger, broader gaze. You are still concerned about your classroom and students but are more likely to consider all options and how they affect everyone in the scenario.

One professor said that his students had just enough knowledge to be dangerous, and this is about the point when that statement is valid. Finishing coursework and thinking about the internship begins to solidify the administrator in you, but do you really want the job?

Sometimes rediscovering the passion that initiated the adventure is necessary to sustain what will come. Remembering why we chose to be leaders in the first place may take a jolt, as this student discovered. (See appendix H, "Traits of Outstanding Leaders," and appendix J, "Conveying a Belief in Self in a Job Interview and Beyond.")

SNAPSHOT 2.3: A TASTE OF LEADERSHIP

When beginning my final internship experience, I made a private deal with myself that if I did not get an assistant principal position that summer, I would not actively pursue an administrative job. After all, I was having second thoughts. I decided I would wait for a sign that this was what I was meant to do. Boy, did I get one!

I returned from a short family vacation to my internship site. I was fortunate to be learning a lot from my mentor there, and we had a tremendous relationship. That morning she asked me to come to her office because she had some news for me. My heart leapt and I just knew that I had received an appointment as an assistant principal. The message was quite different. While I was away three others had been appointed to open positions. These three were not licensed or even enrolled in graduate programs. They were simply pulled from their classrooms and told they would now be assistant principals. I was furious!

Wait, I was furious? Why? Didn't I decide to wait for a sign? Wasn't I happy already? This moment of anger was the sign. It surprised me that I wanted this so much. I was no longer on the fence at this point. I actually felt these individuals had gotten "my job," a job that just a few days earlier I was only lukewarm about. Now I was willing to fight for it!

Eleven interviews and no job later, I felt like a loser. Little did I know that I would soon be catapulted into the world of school leadership in a big way! They called on a Tuesday. Another county, another system, an assistant principalship in a middle school. I took the job.

For this particular student, the passion that prompted beginning a master's program, completing it, and then pursuing a leadership role in a school was reawakened by the threat of not accomplishing the final goal—a job as an assistant principal. No matter what you learned in the graduate program, what accolades or grades you received, it will be this fight, this passion that sees you through. Something inside, perhaps awakened by reading or writing, may be realized by observing great and not-so-great leaders, but it is definitely palpable now. (See appendix H, "Traits of Outstanding Leaders.")

Education is such a personal vocation. Teaching becomes how teachers identify themselves. When taken seriously, as it is by most teachers, teaching is hard work that can be gratifying. The classroom, the students, the lessons . . . is it all left behind when we become administrators?

There is definitely a "mourning phase," most acutely felt in August when there is no room to prepare, no posters to hang, no desks to arrange, nothing to symbolize the beginning of the year. Questions begin to arise: Am I really a leader? What do I know about running a school? Imposter syndrome sets in as we lose who we were as teachers and become who we are as administrators. As described by Arthur Schlesinger Jr. (2000, p. 439): "Although I now rather enjoyed lecturing, I never quite escaped the imposter complex, the fear that I would one day be found out. My knowledge was by some standards considerable, but it was outweighed by my awareness of my ignorance. I always saw myself skating over thin ice."

If this complex was felt by a Pulitzer Prize–winning historian, what it must feel like for most mortals! Teachers become leaders someplace between imposter complex and identity crisis. (See appendix O, "Sources of Power Available to You as an Educational Leader and Decision Maker.")

SNAPSHOT 2.4: WHO AM I NOW?

But would I leave all that I was as a teacher behind? What lessons could I possibly take with me to the assistant principalship? What had I learned in the classroom that would be applicable to the office?

First of all, *some* things came very naturally, like communicating with parents and staff. The relationships I had worked to create within the walls of my classroom with the most difficult parents and students would now be blueprints for creating those relationships on a larger level. Mutual respect and honesty, two things I demanded of and taught my students in my classroom, would become the cornerstone of who I was as a school leader. That was easy.

Next, it was evident that the organization and attention to detail I gave to classroom lesson plans were also transferable to the office. Reports, schedules, and evaluations were all simplified by making a plan and then working the plan. The same principles I had applied to lesson planning were critical to school planning. No problems there.

OK, then, what was missing? Could just anyone do this? I began to take inventory of the skills I used in my English class. Maybe I was more prepared than I thought? All it took was about a week to realize that some of the things I knew as a teacher would be meaningless to me as an assistant principal.

Nothing prepared me to crawl under the Thomas Built bus, crouched in my Jones New York suit, to retrieve a child. No coaxing would bring him out. I never dreamed that my $42,000 degree would eventually qualify me as the only one to plunge the toilets prior to open house. Even my lowest moments did not prepare me to address the death of a student or a staff member. There was a lot I did not know and a lot that I was reminded I did not know on a daily basis.

What was the reason then that I left the classroom, the place where I was at least competent? What promises had I made myself and the students I would affect if I moved into the assistant principalship? (See appendix C, "The Power of Critique.")

Many great teachers "move on" to be assistant principals to make a difference, to affect more classrooms, and to fulfill their own desires to "do it better" than someone else, only to realize that the assistant principal was doing the best he or she could, the same as they will. Doing the best you can involves deciding what you know, what you don't, and, in a sense, leaving part of the expert you've become during your years as a teacher behind and becoming a novice again.

CONCLUSION

"One foot in" means you are still a teacher in your heart, in your routines. You still view the world as a teacher. "One foot out" means you will now have a much broader, more realistic view of the school, community, students, and, hardest of all, colleagues. Some lessons to remember as you begin to balance this "What have I done?" decision follow.

One foot in:

1. Never forget what it is like to be a teacher. This will serve you well as you listen, solve problems, and "stand in the gap" for teachers in your school.
2. Think like the best teacher you ever were when faced with student misbehavior, parent complaints, and teacher evaluations.

3. Continue to teach. Take advantage of "teachable" moments with children and adults. Don't just make the decisions; work for understanding.

One foot out:

1. Now you work for all children, not just the twenty-five in your classroom. Remember that your decisions affect many more students.
2. From hiring to evaluating, only allow teachers you'd want for your own kids to work in your school. This may mean having difficult conversations with folks who worked with you side by side yesterday.
3. As much as you will want to be friends, your job now is to be loyal. Outside any illegal or unethical activity, you must support the principal. This is often lonely, but it will earn you the respect of others in the long run.
4. Remember the reasons you entered school leadership. Write them down, say them out loud, find a circle of friends who are also assistant principals to talk to, but don't forget what brought you to this place.

Now that you have considered ways in which your teacher leadership prepared you to become an assistant principal and have made the commitment to a plan for getting the credentials for becoming a school administrator, you are ready to work the plan. The following chapter makes the case for creating your own inner curriculum while also taking administration courses.

QUESTIONS FOR DISCUSSION

1. If you were asked to describe the upside and downside of your teaching experience to a person considering teaching, what would you say? Please elaborate on each point.
2. How did these factors influence your decision to become a school administrator, if at all?
3. What lessons from your teaching experience do you expect to carry over to school administration? What lessons do you not expect to carry over to school administration?
4. Given your conversations with colleagues and others, what plans do you have for balancing your professional responsibilities as a school administrator with your personal life? If you presently don't have such plans, how might you create plans to deal with this issue?

5. Does the "one foot in, one foot out" metaphor speak to you in any way? If so, please elaborate, perhaps by giving examples from your transition from teaching to the principal certification program.
6. How do the epigraphs at the beginning of the chapter speak to you at this point in your first steps toward becoming a school administrator?

SUGGESTED READINGS

Brubaker, D. L., & Coble, L. D. (2007b). *Teacher renewal: Stories of inspiration to balance your life.* Clemmons, NC: On Track Press.

McCourt, F. (2005). *Teacher man.* New York: Scribner.

Olson, L. (2007, September 12). Getting serious about preparation. *Leading for Learning, Education Week,* S3–S12.

3

Composing a Meaningful Personal Curriculum while Taking Educational Administration Courses

School systems need vigorous imaginative leadership to meet the challenges presented by community change, declining resources, state and federal accountability, and national concern about the quality of education.

—*Catherine Marshall and Richard M. Hooley (2006, p. 14)*

Memory is not meant to cement us in times past. It is meant to enable us to do better now that which we did not do as well before. It is the greatest teacher of them all. In our dreams lies our unfinished work for the world.

—*Joan Chittister (2008, pp. 156 and 136)*

Reflection is nothing less than an internal dialogue with oneself. It is the process of bringing past experiences to a conscious level, analyzing them, and determining better ways to think and behave in the future.

—*Frank McCourt (2005, pp. xxi–xxii)*

We have a deep tendency to see the changes we need to make as being in our outer world, not in our inner world. It is challenging to think that while we redesign the manifest structures of our organizations, we must also redesign the internal structures of our "mental models."

—*Peter Senge (1990, p. xv)*

Curriculum, including the curriculum of educational administration courses and preparatory programs, is usually defined as "the course of study" to be covered by teachers or professors and their students. We refer to this as the "outer curriculum," as it predates the student's reacting and learning from it. "Inner curriculum" is what happens within the learner as he or she creates meaning from exposure to what is going on outside of him or her (Brubaker, 2004, pp. 20–24).

Self-reflection, as described so well by Frank McCourt in one of the epigraphs that introduce this chapter, is the lifeblood of inner curriculum, for it involves self-criticism and self-celebration. It is obvious as we experience the dumbing down of our culture that teachers and school leaders are challenged to give attention to inner curriculum in relation to outer curriculum (Jacoby, 2008).

Reflection, reasoning, and the love of ideas must be reflected in our choices as to what to teach and how to teach it. This is a special challenge in an age of sound bites, texting, tweeting, many television programs aimed at the lowest common denominator, and the like.

We like to think of courses as one of the many forces and experiences that will serve as springboards to learning in your inner curriculum. It almost goes without saying that these courses should be the best they can possibly be in order to serve as an effective springboard.

The distinction between outer curriculum and inner curriculum is captured in the following snapshot.

SNAPSHOT 3.1: LEARNING TO PLAY THE GAME

It was my last semester as an undergraduate and it was time to review lecture notes in order to take the final exam in the World Religions class. During the semester I also had courses in world literature, world drama, and world history. While sitting behind my desk in a rented room, I began connecting insights from the lecture notes in all of these classes. Facts and concepts, parts of a puzzle, came together in a larger framework of knowledge *that I created.*

The next morning I entered the World Religions classroom with a quiet confidence I had not experienced before. I felt like I was on the wings of angels in writing answers to the essay questions before me. I had integrated learning from my four courses in a personally satisfying way. What I didn't realize was that I was in the eye of a perfect storm, one created by questioning the prevailing wisdom of a professor who segmented knowledge for his own instructional purposes.

The following day I received a phone call from the World Religions professor. He asked me to come to his office as soon as possible to discuss the exam. Although he was affable, it was obvious that he was troubled by what I had written. He simply said, "I only wanted you to write about what you had learned in my class." I left his office with an exam grade of C+, what the professor believed was an acceptable compromise between my creative essay and his expectations. It was only in thinking about this later on that I realized that much of what is considered to be a good student is simply knowing how to play the game.

This college student's inner curriculum, a map he had constructed based in part but not totally on the professor's outer curriculum, was discounted by the professor. The dilemma facing the student in the snapshot is described well by Alec Resnick (2007):

The difference between the successful and unsuccessful student is that the successful student has adapted more effectively to the system, to playing the game. The more closely, quickly, and cheerily you can follow the lead of the adults around you, the more successful you will become. This means more and more students are becoming *professional* students earlier and earlier. School is their job. They become the modern aristocrat, the educatocrat. (p. 24)

The research of McCall, Lombardo, and Morrison (1988) gives one hope in thinking about what really matters in school leadership. "In college I used my intellectual skills to get good grades by knowing the right answers. But at work, I found out that knowing the right answer was only 10 percent of the battle. Working with people was the other 90 percent. And we hadn't learned that at school" (p. 22).

This simply makes the case for multiple intelligences (Gardner, 1993, 2000). Social or interpersonal intelligence, a kind of people smartness, is obviously of considerable importance in school administration, something those of us who teach and mentor students in principal preparation programs must keep in mind.

As you go through your courses toward the principal's credential you will sometimes need to reconcile the dissonance between what your instructors expect you to learn and what your inner curriculum is. Knowing the distinction between your inner curriculum and the expectations of those who assess your progress is an important first step in moving forward toward your first administrative position.

Gloria Steinem (1992) described the importance of this distinction: "Hierarchies try to convince us that all power and well-being come from the outside, that our self-esteem depends on obedience and measuring up to their requirements" (pp. 33–34). What conclusion did she reach with regard to this insight? "Self-authority is the single most important radical idea there is, and there is a real hunger for putting the personal and the external back together again" (p. 55). This will be your challenge as you take preparatory courses, do your internship, and in fact compose your career as an educational administrator. (See appendix J, "Conveying a Belief in Self in a Job Interview and Beyond.")

The challenge for principal preparation program leaders and innovative leaders in schools and school systems was framed best by Marshall and Hooley (2006): "What recruitment, selection, reward, and assessment system will ensure that schools hire and train innovators, leaders of reform, builders of school-community integration, and participatory managers?" (p. 16). (See appendix L, "Preparing to Give Leadership to Educational Reform Efforts.")

KEYS TO CREATING YOUR INNER CURRICULUM

The first important thing to know about educators who will influence you and teach you about becoming an effective educational leader is that each of these persons has different talents and experiences from which you can learn. This makes it a challenge for you to have as much information about each person as you can to assess what they can teach you.

There is no substitute for a proactive stance on your part in gathering this information. (See appendix J, "Conveying a Belief in Self in a Job Interview and Beyond.") To sit back and expect the information to come to you is to go through a preparation program with very limited decision-making data. A hesitant applicant for an MSA program describes this pitfall.

SNAPSHOT 3.2: MAKING UP MY MIND

For several years I couldn't "get off the dime" and do something about my future. To be honest, I saw myself as a victim of circumstances. I sometimes thought that my parents' expectations for my brothers were higher than they were for me because I was a girl.

Although my academic record was not distinguished, I made it through my undergraduate program at a good university and managed to be successful as a teacher who was able to reach kids with behavior problems. I identified with them and they knew that I had been where they were now. I was especially successful in reaching young women as their basketball coach. I mentored them through their high school and college years, with a few of them becoming teachers.

I couldn't seem to get the rest of my life in as good order as my teaching. I had friends who seemed to move from one problem to another without solving them. I felt a sense of loyalty to them, but they were pulling me down.

My life seemed to turn around when my little girl was born. She means everything to me. My life, however, was complicated by the fact that I didn't know if I was in love enough with her father to marry him. I did, however, want to be close enough to him for my daughter to have a father. I simply had to put this issue on the back burner until I could get the rest of my life in order.

I knew I wanted to move my career forward and get a master's degree in educational administration. And yet I simply couldn't seem to get my act together enough to apply for the program. As I look back on it now, I realize that I used excuses to stay in the victim role: I had debt from my undergraduate education. A master's degree program would take time away from my daughter. I didn't have the money for tuition and books.

I had come to the point at which I admitted to myself, if not others, that my roots in doubts and fears got me stuck in reasons not to do something. In fact, I was sometimes paralyzed because of my fears. I had come to the place in my life and career where I knew I had to move ahead in spite of my fears. I needed to be consumed with an important mission or project.

Finally, with the encouragement of my mother, my brother, and an aunt who is a teacher, I took the plunge and got into a master's degree program on a probationary basis. The first year of full-time study was tough, as I had a lot of catching up to do, especially with my writing skills. But I learned that success breeds success, and in the process I have gained the confidence, with the help of my student friends and a couple of professors who are kind of like mentors, to begin my second and final year of the master's program.

It is clear to me now that the most difficult step was the first step, having the courage to apply for admission to the program. (See appendix A, "Selecting a School Principal Licensure Program.")

The struggle of the MSA applicant in this snapshot tugs at our hearts, especially the hearts of those of us who have chosen to do the hard work of changing old habits. Janet Rae-Dupree (2008) helps us understand this hard work: "Rather than dismissing ourselves as unchangeable creatures of habit, we can instead direct our own change by consciously developing new habits." She adds: "The more new things we try—the more we step outside our comfort zone—the more inherently creative we become, both in the workplace and in our personal lives" (p. 4). (See appendix G, "A Personal Leadership Change and Conservation Inventory" and appendix F, "Working Alone and Working in a Team.")

Sarason also reminds us that "you cannot create the conditions which enable others to change unless those conditions exist for you" (1972, p. xiv). The personal and the professional go hand in hand. Sarason's words also remind us that settings, like individuals, have their own personalities.

This student's story illustrates the value of a support system and gathering information that she could assess to move forward with her new career path. With regard to your assessment of the information you gather, any judgments you make will depend on your occupational goals and objectives.

For example, one beginning teacher knew from the first day he taught that he wanted to be a superintendent of schools. The clarity of his goal helped him focus on any information he could acquire as to what a superintendent of schools does to be successful and the steps a candidate would have to go through to become a superintendent of schools. This early recognition of his desire to be in such a high-ranking administrative position is in our experience as professors of educational administration quite unusual.

Sue Burgess, who began her career as an assistant principal and moved through the ranks to become superintendent of schools in Virginia and North Carolina, had shorter-range career goals at the onset. She was, however, influenced at an early age with regard to her career goals by a woman superintendent. There were bumps in the road as she made her way through preparatory programs. Her whole story needs to be told in her own words in order to demonstrate the roles of determination and a moral compass, essential ingredients in her inner curriculum (Brubaker & Coble, 2007a, pp. 46–48).

SNAPSHOT 3.3: THE POWER OF AN ADMINISTRATOR AS A ROLE MODEL

When I graduated from Roanoke City Schools, we had a woman superintendent, Dorothy Gibboney, the first woman superintendent in Virginia. This was in the sixties. During my twelve years in the Roanoke City Schools, we had two superintendents, a woman and a man. If you had asked me at age eighteen what percentage of superintendents in our country are women, I would have naively responded, "I guess about 50 percent." (I didn't realize that Dorothy Gibboney was an anomaly.)

The thing that kept my dreams alive is that if I really want to do something, telling me that I can't do it invokes a passionate response. My *internal* voice says, "I'll show him!" The earliest memory of this was when I was a fourth grader in beginning band and took my brother's hand-me-down clarinet to school. Toward the end of the year, the band director approached me in private and said, "Sue, did you say you had a cornet or any other instrument at home that you could switch to? I'm sorry to have to tell you this, but you'll never be able to play a clarinet."

All summer, I kept my secret about his comment, and in the fall, a miraculous thing happened! We got a new band director. When I went back to school to start the fifth grade, I walked in with my clarinet and didn't tell the band director I couldn't play. I pretended that I could play and worked even harder that year. By the time I graduated from high school I was the only person from Roanoke who had been in the All Virginia Band four times. I went on to play in the Roanoke Symphony, the Winston-Salem Symphony, and the Greensboro Symphony.

During the twenty-three months that I sought a job as a superintendent, I applied sixteen times. Six of those times, I was not selected for an interview. Of the ten times that I interviewed, I was chosen as a finalist six times. On four of those six occasions, I was told informally that I had finished second. I started to get a "bridesmaid complex," but like Avis I decided to try harder! I was especially frustrated over gender-related questions like the following:

- How can a woman delegate and follow up to see that the job is done?

- How can a woman check the roads in bad weather to decide whether or not to have school?

- If there is a roof problem, how can a woman check it out?

- If you get this job, what will your husband do? (Brubaker & Coble, 2007a, p. 46)

Sue continued doing good work in her position as a principal until she moved into her first superintendency. Success in that role led to other superintendencies. Her narrative illustrates a second key to creating a personal curriculum—*persistence*! She didn't give up reaching toward her goal of becoming a superintendent of schools. Determination, with an eye on the goal, was a strong source of power in her leadership.

You may encounter naysayers in your preparation program and career as an administrator, but keeping your eye on your goals while working in a persistent and determined way will enhance your personal curriculum platform each step of the way.

It is interesting that Daniel Cobb, chief learning officer for the New York City–based Knowledge Is Power program, "looks for grit and tenacity in an individual's prior working relationships with adults." This is "because principals improve student performance primarily by working with adults, not youngsters. They have to see their role as creating an environment and an organization in which teacher and students can succeed" (Olson, 2007, p. S4).

You may find it helpful to talk to school and school-system administrators about their experiences during the credentialing process. During her first year in an MSA program a student shared the following from a conversation she had with a friend in the principalship. The principal's story is in the following snapshot.

SNAPSHOT 3.4: SOME GOOD ADVICE ON PACING MYSELF

I had the same problem during the middle of my MSA program that I had as a second-year assistant principal. I didn't know how to pace myself. I would try to do too many things at the same time, often wandering from one thing to another without seeming to finish anything well.

I learned that focusing my energies was a key to completing the task at hand. When I felt burned out, I learned to ask myself, "What got me in this depleted condition? What motivated me to run too fast?" I discovered this was a pattern I got into as a child. I simply felt guilty for saying "no" whenever I was asked to do this or that. In high school, for example, I was way overextended in extracurricular activities.

I learned with time that rituals are a beginning step in creating good habits, habits that help a leader stay the course. Setting priorities and saying "no" to many of the things I didn't really want to do, like singing in the church choir and serving on every church committee I was asked to serve on, became rituals that I was comfortable with over time. My mentor during the graduate program said a humorous thing that described my struggle with the pacing issue: "The monkey is off your back but the circus has not left town." I always remind myself of this comment when I am inclined to overextend myself.

We find in our work with students in principal preparation programs and principals in professional development activities that learning to pace oneself is a major challenge. One of the most common reactions we get when we ask the question "When did you learn to pace yourself?" is "I haven't learned to do this yet." Respondents sometimes add, "I will do this when I retire!" We always smile at each other at this point in the conversation.

AN MSA PROGRAM (OUTER CURRICULUM) AND YOUR CHALLENGE IN USING IT AS A SPRINGBOARD FOR COMPOSING YOUR INNER CURRICULUM

As noted in the preface of this book, there has recently been a shift in many principal credentialing programs from a scattershot approach to greater emphasis on the principal's role in curriculum, instruction, student achievement, and research and writing on leadership in general and school leadership in particular. Case studies in which the student solves real-world problems and school-based projects are also used. Frequently, less attention is paid to managerial skills. More rigorous selection and recruitment of candidates are also emphasized in many programs (Olson, 2007, pp. S3–S8).

Principal certification issues are front and center. Supply and demand are a major concern due to principals retiring and leaving for other reasons, such as career advancement and opportunities in other sectors of the economy. Current principal shortages have pushed twenty states to offer alternative principal certification, with estimates that jobs in school administration will grow 10 to 20 percent in the next five years.

State and local requirements vary, with some arguing that national requirements are also necessary. There are different views as to the shelf life of principal certification endorsements and the number of years, if any, of teaching experience required.

The question of conditional or probationary admissions has also been raised, with some arguing that no probation is necessary if a candidate has had a successful internship. This also introduces the question of what constitutes a successful internship.

Security requirements and background checks of applicants introduce matters of transparency and privacy. Plagiarism and enhancement of resumes become related issues that must be addressed at state and local levels.

What kind of testing procedures or principal certification exams, if any, should be required of applicants? Some argue that no written or oral examination is valid. What should be the relationship between evaluation and measurement? Is measurement (the use of numbers) one kind of evaluation, or are measurement and evaluation one and the same? What kinds of qualitative evaluation of principal certification candidates should be considered?

Should principal certification be transferable from state to state or limited to the state in which it is originally given? And should there be separate certification, or should it be tied to a master's degree?

The national standards movement in school administration has had a significant influence on programs of study for those who wish to enter the profession. Those who presently want to improve standards for school leaders stand on the shoulders of earlier pioneers, such as Neil Shipman and Joseph Murphy. In 1996, the Interstate School Leaders Licensure Consortium (ISLLC) published its *Standards for School Leaders*. Personnel from twenty-four state education agencies and representatives from various professional organizations presented a common core of knowledge, dispositions, and performances to reinvent leadership for schools.

In 2008, the ISLLC published *Educational Leadership Policy Standards*, which was adopted by the National Policy Board for Educational Administration. The six standards read as follows.

> Standard 1: An education leader promotes the success of every student by facilitating the development, articulation, implementation, and stewardship of a vision of learning that is shared and supported by all stakeholders.
>
> Standard 2: An educational leader promotes the success of every student by advocating, nurturing, and sustaining a school culture and instructional program conducive to student learning and staff professional growth.
>
> Standard 3: An education leader promotes the success of every student by ensuring management of the organization, operation, and resources for a safe, efficient, and effective learning environment.

Standard 4: An education leader promotes the success of every student by collaborating with faculty and community members, responding to diverse community interests and needs, and mobilizing community resources.

Standard 5: An education leader promotes the success of every student by acting with integrity, fairness, and in an ethical manner.

Standard 6: An education leader promotes the success of every student by understanding, responding to, and influencing the political, social, economic, legal, and cultural context.

The ISLLC tried to lend more specificity to each of the standards by identifying functions that were still of a somewhat generalized nature. For example, the first function under Standard 1 reads as follows: "Collaboratively develop and implement a shared vision and mission." Therefore, as the ISLLC standards were used in the licensure test, universities, and the licensing agencies, their relevancy was often questioned due to their general nature.

The challenge for school-system leaders and school leaders is how to translate the standards into the management of schools. All recognize that putting standards into practice is a tough job. Interpretation of the standards is the key. Leaders tend to cherry-pick in order to serve their own political purposes.

To some, the standards are a useful tool to compose case studies of present practices. They are benchmarks that give practitioners a sense of direction.

To others, standards are questionable, if not counterproductive. These others warn that conformity and uniformity should not be confused with excellence. Creative leaders, it is argued, will be driven away from school and school-system administration if expected to paint by the numbers.

There is another professional development movement for principals being implemented that will have implications for you as you move into an assistant principalship. After years of discussion, the creation of an advanced national certification program for principals is underway.

The new program builds on the National Board's twenty-year certification program for teachers and school counselors. It emphasizes instructional leadership, organizational change, and community involvement, with the principal's role in school management as a central core.

The launching of National Board Certification for Principals was joined by Education Secretary Arne Duncan on December 8, 2009, at the National Press Club in Washington, DC.

The National Board for Professional Teaching Standards (NBPTS) is a voluntary performance-based assessment program. It is an independent, non-profit, nonpartisan, and nongovernmental organization that will invite your participation. It will be to your advantage to pay attention to this professional development certification program as it evolves in the near future.

The MSA program in the Department of Educational Leadership and Cultural Foundations at the University of North Carolina at Greensboro will be used to illustrate a principal credentialing program. (See www.uncg.edu/elc/msa.html, pp. 1–2.) It is designed to prepare students for leadership and administration at the school building level and specifically for positions as principals and assistant principals. The degree leads to North Carolina Level I administrator licensure (school principal).

Entrance requirements for admission to the MSA program are a grade point average of 3.0 or better during the last half of the bachelor's degree and an acceptable score on the Graduate Record Exam or Miller's Analogy Test. However, admissions decisions are based on an applicant's full set of application materials, including work experience, recommendations and letters of reference, and the individual's personal statement. Admissions officers try to remind themselves that "achievement is talent plus preparation" (Gladwell, 2008, p. 39).

The MSA program is a forty-two-semester-hour graduate program. It consists of ten three-semester-hour courses and twelve credits of internship. Courses are offered in the evenings during the fall on campus or as online courses. The time allowed for obtaining the degree is five years after the first date, but extensions are sometimes possible. Most students are part-time students who typically take two courses per term (including during the summer semester). Classes are frequently scheduled so that many students can take two classes in one evening.

The following educational leadership courses are required.

ELC 615: Foundations of Curriculum

ELC 616: Culturally Relevant Leadership

ELC 660: The School Principalship

ELC 662: Power, Politics, and Schools

ELC 670: Leadership for Teaching and Learning

ELC 673: Principal Leadership for Special Education

ELC 675: Schools as Centers of Inquiry (a research course)

ELC 684: Teacher Rights, Responsibilities, and Evaluation

ELC 687: Legal and Ethical Dimensions of Leadership

ELC 691: School Organization and Leadership

Considerable discussion among department faculty in general and professors teaching the MSA courses in particular has led to changes in course titles and content. These changes may be summarized as follows, after which the implications for MSA students' construction of their own inner curricula will be discussed.

Not only are MSA programs working to be responsive to student needs while developing meaningful curricula, but as licensure programs they also balance state requirements and standards, which may or may not be congruent. Sometimes it's difficult to reconcile what you want as a student, what the state requires, and what the department faculty deem relevant.

Sitting in on capstone hearings for graduating students is especially enlightening. It can be a time of great reflection, not only for the student but for the faculty as well. Professors always ask students at the end of the hearing, "What is it that you would change about the program?" It never fails—students always respond in one way or another that they wish they had more "practical" experience during their preparation. When asked to be specific, they often list budget and scheduling as items left out of their preparation experience. More "hands on," more "real life" instead of theory is what they want.

What they *mean* is that they are in survival mode as new administrators. They have to get the schedule out and get the budget right in a particular time frame. Survival looks different to them from what they have considered in their classes. Nothing they've read or discussed in class comes to mind when responding to the demand of the assistant superintendent about why the budget is $25,000 out of whack.

The fact of the matter is that what is missing is the application of what has been learned, not how practical or useful it may or may not have been. What is missing is the time it takes to really think about the task and what learning can be transferred to that task. New administrators always list time as a barrier for everything from dealing with student misbehavior in a way that makes sense to affecting real change in schools. They always feel like their heads are just above water and that there is a lot the university did not do to prepare them for the day-to-day responsibilities and decision making that goes on in the office.

Constructing a meaningful personal curriculum depends on making connections and being reflective. At the University of North Carolina at Greensboro, generally, students begin the MSA program with ELC 660: The School Principalship. The description of the course states, "Functions in providing a system of communications, organizing people to meet educational goals, defining and formulating goals and objectives, leadership in instruction, supervision, curriculum design and development, personnel administration, and ethical and legal responsibilities."

Students may also take ELC 670: Leadership for Teaching and Learning, a course that "examines conceptions of 'good' schools and the nature of instruction, curriculum, assessment, and professional development and explores leadership, change, and school renewal work toward good schooling and pedagogy." These courses set the stage for the next two to three years of coursework and challenge students to think about what the principalship looks like from the inside out instead of the outside in.

As students progress, they question what skills they will need to succeed in the role of school leader or administrator. Complicating matters is the fact that success is not defined solely by the university but also by the state and the district in which the student serves or wishes to serve. Sometimes these definitions of success are inconsistent and the student must discern what learning will best position them in the school district they desire.

The inner curriculum is shaped by many forces, some in direct conflict. Universities defend their curriculum as "important," states defend their standards as essential, and districts require administrators who are competent according to their values. Students get caught in the middle.

Important to remember is the internal guide that directed you to leadership in the first place. Where you stand and what you learn will always be personal—somewhere in the mix—not a product of the university you attend, the state you live in, or the district that employs you, but of the person you are and the leader you become in the process. Don't lose sight of that.

In conclusion, the importance of the inner curriculum for aspiring school administrators, those presently in school administrative positions, teachers, and students can't be overemphasized. It is incumbent on those of us who work in preservice and in-service administrator education to recognize and help our aspiring school administrators connect inner curriculum with outer curriculum in our principal preparation programs.

Our own attitudes and behaviors, particularly with respect to conversations with aspiring school administrators on this matter, are especially crucial. The principal preparation curricula we create should reflect our views on the relationship between inner curriculum and more formal areas of study.

In working with aspiring school administrators, we can set an example in seeking a balance between emphasis on inner curriculum and outer curriculum. Our inner curriculum shouldn't be rigid and inflexible. Rather, we should have an open mind and willingness to treat knowledge as proximate rather than final. We should also create the best outer curriculum we can so that it serves as a useful and stimulating springboard for inner curricula. It is important for you, a person considering entering a principal certification program or a person already in such a program, to be up-to-date on certification issues discussed in this chapter and the role of national, state, and local organizations in shaping such issues. Your professional development leaders and mentors can be a key resource in giving you relevant information. It is up to you to adopt a proactive stance in order to acquire such information.

It is during the internship that you will get closer to the real world of school administration. The internship is a place where you will begin to practice reconciling forces in order to find balance in your professional life. The internship is the subject of the next chapter in this book.

QUESTIONS FOR DISCUSSION

1. Have you previously considered the distinction between "inner curriculum" and "outer curriculum" discussed at the beginning of this chapter? What difference can this distinction make in your professional life at this time?

2. F. Scott Fitzgerald (1936), Irish-American novelist and short-story writer, observed that "the test of a first-rate intelligence is the ability to hold two opposed ideas in the mind at the same time and still retain the ability to function." What contradictions have you experienced as a teacher and how

have you reconciled them in order to function? What contradictions have you experienced as a graduate student in a principal preparation program? For example, how do you reconcile some student-measurement assessments with expectations that you will consider variances in the personal growth of students? Or how will you build what you consider to be necessary "wiggle room" into seemingly inflexible rules and regulations regarding student discipline?

3. Have you been told, as Sue Burgess was in snapshot 3.3, that certain career opportunities are simply not open to you? How did you react to this in terms of your feelings and actions? Have you observed others who have been in this situation? What have they done? What would you have done if you had been in their places?

4. What role models have been important to you as a teacher and aspiring school administrator? What have you learned from their examples? For example, some principals encourage teachers who show signs of leadership by volunteering and/or accepting club sponsorships or student government adviserships to think about administration.

5. How would you compare and contrast the master's program in educational administration described in this chapter with the one in which you are enrolled? Please be as specific as possible in answering this question.

6. How do the epigraphs at the beginning of this chapter speak to you as you take your first steps in becoming a school administrator?

SUGGESTED READINGS

Brubaker, D. L., & Coble, L. D. (2005). *The hidden Leader: Leadership lessons on the potential within.* Thousand Oaks, CA: Corwin Press. See chapter 9, "The power of determination," 135–46.

Hess, F. M., & Kelly, A. P. (2005). "The accidental principal." *Education Next, 5*(3), 34–40.

———. (2007). "Learning to lead: What gets taught in principal preparation programs." *Teachers College Record, 109*(1), 244–74.

Olson, L. (2007, September 12). "Getting serious about preparation." *Leading for Learning, Education Week,* S3–S12.

4

Negotiating a Successful Internship

John Dewey pointed out eons ago, there are two kinds of knowing: Knowledge we have gained on a conceptual level, and knowledge based on concrete experience, which becomes part of your psychological bloodstream.

—*Seymour Sarason (2002, p. 6)*

The secret to success in school and in life is *meaningful work*—"the miracle of meaningful work."

—*Malcolm Gladwell (2008, p. 269)*

Wisdom is what lasts after an experience ends.

—*Joan Chittister (2008, p. 124)*

The internship. The practical, on-the-job experience. The reality of serving in a school or school system is vital to the development of leaders. It almost creeps up on you as you complete coursework. An internship is defined as an official or formal program to provide practical experience. It is the time when you test all you've learned in the classroom. It's the time when you see theory in action and think to yourself, "This stuff really happens." This is the fun part, if you choose right.

Your current role in the school or district will significantly impact how your internship plays out. If you are a classroom teacher, you will negotiate an internship with the chief administrator at your school. This internship will consist of activities that are conducted outside your regular duties, occurring mostly during planning periods, before school, or after school.

If you are a counselor, curriculum facilitator, or are in another quasi-administrative role, you may have more flexibility in internship activities during the day as your schedule allows. Some students even complete the internship while serving as assistant principal. In this case, your job *is* your internship.

Fewer students have the opportunity to complete the internship as a full-time student intern. In this case, a prior relationship with the school or district is capitalized upon or the student creates a connection during formal and informal shadowing visits in a school. Despite the different paths, there is no question that the internship is crucial to the development of the student as a leader.

THE POWER OF CHOICES

Making the right choice for the internship is critical. Being certain that you will learn from a "master," gain powerful knowledge, engage in authentic activities, and create a meaningful relationship with your internship mentor are all great goals, but the first step is securing the internship itself. No problem, right? An intern is, in essence, free labor. Everyone wants one. Right? Wrong!

SNAPSHOT 4.1: NOBODY WANTS ME

"My principal won't sign my internship application. What else can I do?" The conversation started badly. As an internship advisor, the issue came up not often, but often enough that I knew there was some reason the principal would not commit to the internship. The student needed twelve hours and was frantic, but as a former principal myself, I understood that there must be another issue here.

There had to be something behind the principal's response: that he was afraid that the internship hours would interfere with teaching and supervisory duties already assigned. Now I was in the middle. I felt compelled to advocate for the student but could identify with the school-based administrator and his reluctance to take on the role of site-based supervisor for this student, who was a teacher in the school.

Forming relationships that will facilitate your placement as an intern is vital. Students often underestimate how their performance in the classroom or interactions with peers will affect their ability to bargain for a substantial internship later. They do not realize that every interaction may impact their ability or inability to be placed, even in their own schools.

A student recently said, "It may be difficult to place me. I've worked for so many principals and burned bridges everywhere I worked." Unfortunately, the leadership potential of this student may be overshadowed by the "back-stage" information being shared in the administrator network in his school district. Relationships are paramount—more far-reaching than any grade you make in graduate school, more powerful than any presentation you ever give. Relationships will open the door for you to show what you can do. Without positive ones, you will not move forward. (See appendix H, "Traits of Outstanding Leaders.")

Now you're in. You have maintained or created the conditions sufficient to secure an internship. What now? Your next steps will be important in not only *being* successful but also *feeling* successful.

Internship means something different to everyone. As a student, you may have very specific ideas about what you will do as an intern. The picture you create in your mind may be very different from the one the site supervisor has created. Your expectations may be to simply observe what happens all day while the principal supervising you envisions you suspending students the first day.

Navigating what the internship will look like is crucial. Sitting down with the site supervisor and brainstorming a list of daily internship activities you will engage in along with larger-scale projects that you might assume responsibility for will alleviate misunderstandings down the road. Better yet, write it all down. Create a memorandum of understanding or a job description for the internship. If this step is ignored, the internship can go wrong really fast, as captured in the reflections of this principal and intern. They are obviously not on the same page. Wrong page, wrong book.

SNAPSHOT 4.2: PRINCIPAL AND INTERN HAVE VERY DIFFERENT VIEWS

As a principal, I have a tremendous workload. The thought of having an extra hand this year was great. Who knew that taking on a full-time intern would be a full-time job? He visited me twice last year, made a good impression, asked all the right questions, and seemed eager to "get his hands dirty," so I signed his application and looked forward to having him on bus duty in August.

Little did I know how needy he would be. He is never on time. Even if he did arrive on time, I never know what days to expect him. Sometimes he comes all week; sometimes I never see him. When he does show up, he never seems to know what to do, hanging around in the office until he is given explicit directions. I do not have time for this. I do not have time to make a list of what needs to be done. Isn't part of leadership seeing what needs to be done and doing it? I feel more like a babysitter than anything else. Now he wants me to fill out an evaluation form for him. Evaluation of what? I haven't seen him do anything. He certainly has not taken initiative!

* * *

As an intern, I am stressed out. At first, the thought of working with this principal seemed great. She seemed so together when I visited her twice last year. I asked questions and thought I impressed her with the research I did on the school. She did not even give me a schedule. I came in the whole first week of school but felt like I was in the way. She'd tell me what to do if she saw me but gave no specific instructions. I know she is a perfectionist, so I am worried about jumping in and making a mess of things.

* * *

The student is thinking one thing and the supervisor another. Neither has a very positive image of the other. The whole situation could have been avoided in the beginning with a frank conversation about expectations. It is the student's responsibility to initiate this conversation, not the site supervisor's.

While the person agreeing to supervise your internship in the field may "sign off," he or she may not fully understand exactly what this means. Some universities have mentor-training programs or lists of suggested activities, but it is ultimately your professional obligation to establish clear roles and responsibilities at the outset. Confusion and hard feelings about unmet expectations are not desired outcomes of your intern experience.

It is during the internship that the realities of educational administration in general and the assistant principalship in particular are introduced to the intern. One of these realities came to our attention while supervising an intern who was an excellent student but outspoken in her relationships with others at the university and in the school where she was an intern. What she learned is best described in her own words.

SNAPSHOT 4.3: LEARNING TO WATCH
WHAT I SAY AND TO WHOM

I was raised in a large family where we freely expressed our feelings. As I think about it, it became "part of my charm" with my friends and others, who laughed at some of the ways I described situations in which I found myself. This was even true when I became a teacher. My colleagues got a kick out of the humorous way I talked about experiences I had with my students and others, and I must admit that some of my comments had a bite to them.

As an intern I was placed in a school that had a significant achievement gap that the newly assigned principal was addressing. I respected this principal for her professionalism and actually saw her as a kind of role model I wanted to emulate. She gave me the assignment of working with a seasoned assistant principal to gather student data requested by central office.

I dug in and worked for some time with the assistant principal, to the point where I actually was both tired and bored. At the end of one day, I turned to him and said, "How do you put up with all of this *scut work*?" I noticed a strange expression on his face but didn't think much about it.

A few days later the principal asked me to drop by her office, and I immediately knew that something was wrong. This is basically what she said:

"You are bright, hardworking, and a good intern, but there is something that you need to give attention to as you move into administration. A few days ago you said something to the assistant principal that troubled him. You referred to his job as *scut work*. The word itself and the way you said it was demeaning. It discounted the importance of his work. It was especially insensitive as he is a person who has been an assistant principal for several years and takes his job seriously. This is an opportunity for you to learn that as an administrator you need to give attention to what you say and to whom. Teachers can get away with saying things at the supermarket and with colleagues that can cost assistant principals or principals dearly if they say them. I'll help you work on this as it's important to learn."

I knew that what the principal told me was true. I apologized and said that I would address the issue. I followed up by apologizing to the assistant principal. It was a hard lesson to learn, but I knew that this was something I needed to change in order to be a successful principal.

Being outspoken is one thing, but at least the spoken word fades. During the internship it is important to begin to consider the public persona you are creating. You are becoming a representative of the school, the district, and the community. What you "publish" and "archive" is reflective of a greater entity than just you. While the spoken word does not last forever, what you write, text, or e-mail becomes written history.

Though while you were in the classroom it may not have occurred to you to be vigilant about your written communications, the internship is the time to truly think before you write, and writing is texting and e-mailing. We have become so comfortable with these modes of communication that often they are regarded as the spoken word, but make no mistake, an e-mail or a text is a written document. The ease with which we send messages lulls us into the belief that they are just a conversation, but anything in writing is documentation.

There is a difference, one you do not have to consider when you are not a representative of the larger community and its standards. The power of the written word can be saved, shared, and revisited, thus reigniting any emotions evoked by the initial interaction. Unfortunately, the intern described in the following snapshot did not realize how a seemingly simple mistake would derail his career forever.

SNAPSHOT 4.4: "ZIPPING" OFF AN E-MAIL

Supervising interns is always rewarding, but every now and then you get one who just doesn't get it, an intern who is so confident and so sure he knows everything that there is really nothing you can tell him. While I appreciate self-confidence, I also encourage my interns to be a little humble, to realize they do not know everything. Even if they would do things differently, they can learn from those who are experienced. Usually, there is one event that turns the tables. In this case, it was an e-mail.

The intern was assigned a grade level in a large, affluent high school. He was given the tasks of a regular assistant principal, including student discipline and parent contact. The guy was really capable but rarely stopped to think or confer with others, convinced he had all the answers and too arrogant to ask for guidance.

I remember the call.

"I screwed up," he said. He sounded like he was on the verge of tears. He went on to tell me that a parent had e-mailed him about her son.

"OK," I prompted. "Then what?"

"What I meant to do was forward the e-mail to a buddy of mine."

What he had really done was say some nasty things about the child and sent the e-mail to the parent instead. Needless to say, the principal had a mess to clean up, and the parent had more than a recollection of a verbal interchange. She had documentation of the unkind, unprofessional words of the intern regarding her son.

That intern quietly returned to the classroom and never sought a position as an assistant principal. "The e-mail incident" cost him dearly. The principal would not recommend him, the parent was vocal and powerful, and, most of all, there was a written record of his tragic mistake.

Be careful with e-mail and texts. There is something more formal about what is in writing. It lasts forever . . . longer than words hang in the air. This kind of advice is important during the internship and also carries over to the assistant principalship.

A middle school principal in Portland, Oregon, has strong words of advice for school administrators that can save angst. "Never, ever leave a message on an answering machine or send an e-mail that has any detail in it about a student problem." He adds, "Verbal or written messages can be misconstrued and used against the sender. Only leave simple messages asking the parent to return the call."

Social networks like Facebook and MySpace have also added a layer to public perception. Many districts are implementing or considering policies that govern employees' participation in such sites. As an administrative intern, it is imperative to know the current policy of your district and to follow it. Furthermore, understand the implications of living your life online and how it will impact your ability to behave as a leader in the school in which you intern. Photographs or comments that portray you as irresponsible will not contribute to your effectiveness in administration.

In conclusion, the internship is a perfect time to clean up your act, if necessary. You are becoming a public figure, a role model for children, families, and other educators. A good rule of thumb is to eliminate anything that diminishes the respect others may eventually have for you and the work you do in schools. (See appendix B, "The 'Table Manners' of Graduate Student Leadership in a Principal Preparation Program.") If you follow this advice, you will be ready to seek an administrative position, probably as an assistant principal. This is the subject of the following chapter.

QUESTIONS FOR DISCUSSION

1. If you have not experienced being an intern in school administration, what do you anticipate the internship will be like? If you have already been an intern in school administration, what did you think it would be like before you became an intern? In this case, were your expectations realistic? Please give specific examples.
2. If you have been an intern, did you make efforts to find out about the internship before you experienced it? If you haven't been an intern, what are you doing to find out about the internship?

3. Are you aware of the advantages of being proactive in finding out the expectations of the administrator with whom you will work? If you have already been an intern, were you aware of the advantages of being proactive before you became an intern? Please give specific examples.

4. What are the advantages of writing down the role the administrator with whom you will work expects you to play? If you have already been an intern, did you give attention to this at the appropriate time in your relationship with the experienced administrator?

5. What role will your internship supervisor play in the internship process? If you have already been an intern, what role did he or she play? Do you or did you anticipate areas of agreement and disagreement with the supervisor during the internship? Give concrete examples.

6. What have you learned in your professional career with regard to watching what you say and to whom? What guidelines do you have for dealing with this matter during the internship? What guidelines, if any, did you have, if you have already served as an intern?

7. What have you learned about the use of social networks, e-mails, texts, and the like as a teacher? How will you apply your findings to the internship experience and being an assistant principal and principal?

8. How do the epigraphs at the beginning of this chapter speak to you during your first steps in becoming a school administrator?

SUGGESTED READINGS

Gladwell, M. (2008). *Outliers: The story of success.* New York: Little, Brown & Co.

Marshall, C., & Hooley, R. M. (2006). *The assistant principal: Leadership choices and Challenges.* Thousand Oaks, CA: Corwin Press. See chapter 5, "A new and different assistant principalship."

Seeking a Position as an Assistant Principal

The worse you feel, the better you should look.

—Joe Klein (2002, p. 116). A comment Mandy Frunwald, media advisor to Bill Clinton, made in the 1992 New Hampshire primary.

And if you sing though as angels, and love not the singing, you muffle man's ears to the voices of the day and the voices of the night.

—Kahlil Gibran (1923, p. 28)

Patrick Moynihan, a social scientist, understood that social science tells us not what to do but what is not working.

—George Will (2008, p. H6)

Leaders bring their "person" to the practice of leadership. Matching the context of leadership to the "person" of the individual is important to the success of the leader.

—North Carolina Standards for School Executives, 2007

Presentation of self is at the center of seeking an assistant principalship, or any other position as an educational administrator and leader. The question then becomes, "How can I improve my presentation of self attitudes and behaviors to better my chances of getting the administrative position I want?"

Answering this question begins with self-assessment: "What have I learned from my educational experiences in general and my engagement in the principal preparation program in particular that principals and others in the hiring process will like enough to hire me?"

NETWORKING

Networking, the developing of contacts and information, is usually cited as the key process that will lead to employment opportunities. Who do you know in the school(s) or school system(s) you are interested in who can influence the educators who are in on the hiring process? Also, who do you know who knows someone in the school(s) or school system(s) you are interested in who can influence those who might hire you? These key people can help set the stage, or what some call the anticipatory set, so that those involved in the hiring process will be inclined to appreciate what you have to offer.

Who might some of these influential educators be? Professors and instructors in your principal preparatory program, principals and other administrators in the school and school system where you taught, principals and other administrators you got to know during your internship, and one or more mentors who know and appreciate your abilities.

Ask these influential people if they will put in a good word on your behalf and let them choose the best vehicle to use to contact those involved in the hiring process. Some will prefer a more formal process, such as a letter or a recommendation form. Others will prefer to use more informal means, such as a telephone call, note, e-mail, or conversation.

Hopefully, your supporters will highlight your interest in the position, your energy level, your positive attitude, your organizational skills, your ability to deal with conflict, your loyalty to those you work for, your ability to get along with colleagues, your team-building talent, your computer and technology skills, your special expertise as evidenced by success in previous positions, and your public relations skills. In short, they will make the case that you are both competent and qualified to be an assistant principal. (See appendix M, "How Good (and Comfortable) Are You as a Public Speaker and Listener?")

APPLYING FOR AND INTERVIEWING FOR
THE ASSISTANT PRINCIPALSHIP

Applying for an assistant principalship is like searching for any other job: it *is* a full-time job and it is one that begins before it is time to go to work. As stated before, draw on the connections you created in your internship and do your homework. These are the two best pieces of advice we can give.

Create your professional reference list. Think of school leaders for whom you have worked, including the current one. Think of university professors who can speak to your leadership potential and abilities. Think of district-level leaders with whom you have worked on projects or initiatives.

Choosing at least three references is a good rule of thumb. Do this before you apply anywhere. Make sure to ask if it is OK to provide a person's name for a reference. Some individuals may not feel they know you well enough to provide a reference, or some may feel that they cannot provide positive information about your abilities. It's important to know this prior to completing an application. Furthermore, we consider it rude to provide a name and contact information without permission. Catching a potential reference off-guard is not a good idea!

Prepare your references to do the best job for you. Be certain to provide each reference with an updated resume and a job description of the position you seek. (See appendix Q, "Sample Candidate Resume.") This way, each reference can speak specifically about your strengths for that particular position. Make sure references are aware of the jobs you are seeking and that human resource representatives may contact them.

Some individuals prefer to provide a letter or written response instead of doing phone conversations. As the applicant, it is your responsibility to find out what the school district wants and what your references are most comfortable with. Neglecting this step could result in weak references and no interviews.

Now that you have completed the task of identifying those individuals who will promote you officially, begin to research vacancies in school districts. By research, we mean look at the district critically to be certain it is a place where you are willing to work. Look at board policies, district mission and vision, news from that district, district organization, and anything else that will give you an overview of what the district values and will have you promote as a leader in that district.

If it "feels" wrong, don't apply. Many times graduates are only concerned with finding a job when actually finding a fit is the most critical thing. Do not interview for a job you are not willing to take. Furthermore, don't even apply. The following snapshot illustrates the dilemma faced by an interviewee.

SNAPSHOT 5.1: WHY APPLY IF I CAN'T ANSWER THIS QUESTION?

Interviewing for an assistant principalship in a small rural district was what I thought I wanted. I knew the district and the schools pretty well and believed I could contribute to the mission of the district and the growth of students. *What I did not take time to find out was what this particular school really believed.*

I answered the questions appropriately. They were pretty standard: Why do you want to be an assistant principal? Describe your teaching experiences. What are your strengths and weaknesses? Some scenarios were thrown in by the five-person panel, all of whom had smiled and nodded throughout the interview. Things like, "If the bus driver called in sick at 6:45 in the morning, what would you do?" It was actually the answer to that question that sealed the job for me. I answered that I would hop on the bus and drive the route myself. The panel regarded me approvingly, then moved on to the last question. It was then that I wished I had never applied for the job.

A teacher, probably a veteran who had great power in the school, looked at me through squinted eyes and asked me the deal breaker, "How do you feel about corporal punishment?" I knew I could answer with a lie pretty easily and impress the panel. I knew I could *say* that I would beat children when the teachers sent them to my office and never have a problem with it, but I also knew that even if I said I would do it to get the job, I would be lying. Most of all, I did not want to work in a school where that was obviously the expectation, that I would beat children. The job was mine. It hinged on this one answer.

I really wished I had never applied at all. I wished I had known that they believed this so I could have steered clear. Now, no matter what I decided, I lost. If I answered the way they wanted, I would never follow through, thus losing credibility once on the job. If I answered that I did, in fact, have a problem with corporal punishment, then I had wasted their time even interviewing. It was a no-win situation.

Finding a fit is crucial. It begins with the first application you complete. A wise superintendent once said, "Do not apply for a job you are not willing to take that day." Graduates apply haphazardly just trying to find a job when what they really should be doing is finding the right job. The right job will make a difference. Finding it means a deliberate search for a school system that will allow you to be authentic in your work. Better to investigate prior to applying than to find out you have made a mistake.

Once you have established your reference list and done your homework, you are ready to apply. Follow the application procedures for the school system to which you are applying. Do not assume that because you have applied to one system that that process is the same for all. Update applications often and keep copies of everything. Make sure you are completely honest on all application documents, as even a mistake may be regarded as deliberate dishonesty.

In some states, falsifying application documents is even grounds for revocation of a professional license. While we trust no one would purposely do this, close scrutiny of dates and experience is very important. (See appendix Q, "Sample Candidate Resume.")

References are in place, and you have researched and applied for positions; now it's time to create a support system. Think of all the administrators you came in contact with during your graduate work and the internship. Who spoke in your classes? Who did you shadow? Who did you speak with at the principals' monthly meeting while visiting as an intern?

All of these interactions can come into play as you seek a position. Literally sit down and make a list of everyone you know in school or district leadership positions. Find out where these people are now and in what position they serve. If you decide to apply in their district, contact them, remind them who you are, and just let them know you are interested in serving in their school system. You don't have to be a stalker, but keep your name out there any way you can. This may open the door for an interview.

To be invited for an interview is a very positive step in the interviewing process. It is important to keep this in mind in order to build up and keep your confidence during the interview itself. "I can do it" becomes "I will do it well or they wouldn't have even bothered to schedule the interview." (See appendix J, "Conveying a Belief in Self in a Job Interview and Beyond.")

Will you probably experience some nervousness? Yes, and it is important to see this as a natural thing that can work to your advantage. We recommend that you say to yourself, "I care enough about this position as assistant principal and the interviewing committee to have an edge on." We were on one interviewing committee where a committee member made an interesting observation when the candidate left the room at the end of the interview: "Something was wrong with this candidate and I will tell you what it is. He appeared to have no nervousness at all—something that isn't natural. Doesn't he want the job? What is the story anyway?"

The first step in being interviewed is preparation. You will want to know as much as you can about the single interviewer and/or members of the interviewing committee and the school district. You will also want information on the place where you will be interviewed. Make notes about major initiatives taking place and how you can contribute to those initiatives.

A major part of the preparation process is building a frame or view of your strengths that you will bring to the assistant principalship for which you are being interviewed. This frame will show the interviewer(s) how you have organized experiences that have prepared you for this position (Goffman, 1974). This will also demonstrate that you know yourself and are comfortable with yourself as a fit for the position. (See appendix I, "Job Interviewing and the Creation of Learning Communities.")

You will be wise to outline key points in your frame. The following serves as an example.

"I have taught successfully in this setting or one like it and discovered that students will benefit from a firm but fair leadership style. When they were 'out of line' I took appropriate action and then made sure I was in their company sometime later in the day to demonstrate that I accepted them even though I didn't accept their action earlier in the day."

"I see the large picture but also know that 'the devil is in the details.' These details must be attended to, but I don't get lost in them. For example, I wrote a major part of our school's accreditation report but learned that sharing this report to the faculty in a conversational way was as important as the hard copy that I wrote."

"I learned, particularly during my internship, that it is important to listen to and understand teachers' points of view, but it is also true that my role as an assistant principal will lead me to a different point of view. My work on the scheduling of classes and assignment of students to teachers especially taught me this."

The three examples above also demonstrate the importance of speaking clearly and to the point, particularly with respect to the answering of questions during the interviewing process. The more you speak, the more "red flags" are likely to be raised. You will also increase the chances that they will like you by smiling at appropriate times and looking directly at the interviewer(s) when you speak. You will be able to read the verbal and nonverbal cues of the interviewer(s), thus telling you if they feel relaxed and comfortable around you. An affinity connection will have been established.

It should be added that both parties to the interview will be assessing each other's energy levels. Flattened affect on one side or the other will be highly detrimental, thus leaving the negotiation process dead in the water. People will know from your energy level if you love life and want to be with them. (See appendix H, "Traits of Outstanding Leaders.")

Richard Amme (2007), CEO of Amme & Associates, Inc., a media and crisis-management organization, advises candidates "to build on your natural strengths and not try to remake your personality." He believes that "if your decisions are appropriate, you believe in them, and are confident, then your body language and delivery will tend to take care of themselves." In other words, a good message delivered authentically is the key to success. At the same time, Jack and Suzy Welch (2008) advise leaders in large organizations, particularly those who tend to be introverts, to speak up and get out front or risk being overlooked (p. 92).

You will surely be asked if you have any questions for the interview team. One certain way to keep from being overlooked is to be ready with some specific questions. It is never a good idea to respond by saying you do not have questions. This shows a lack of interest on your part. Do not ask about pay, vacation, or work hours. Do ask about specific programs, initiatives, or community strengths.

This is not the time to point out that the school has not made growth in student achievement or that they have a poor community reputation. It is a time to construct questions that will show that you are willing to work on any areas of need or to support any strong points of the school or district. For example, instead of saying, "How do you plan to increase the reading proficiency of your students with disabilities?" you might say, "I hope to build on the work you have already done with students with disabilities. I see from the data provided on your district report card that reading has increased by 10 percent over the past year. To what do you attribute this growth?"

It is always wise to follow up as soon as you can by writing the interviewer or interviewers expressing appreciation for the interview. This makes it clear that you are serious in seeking the assistant principalship in question. We have also found it helpful to drop a line to or call the receptionist/executive assistant who greeted you before the interview. This often-overlooked person is in a position to make a positive difference for you.

Finally, the interviewing process is a two-way street. You are being looked over and assessed by the school and school system and you in turn are doing the same to them. If rapport is established, you will move on to the next step, which will include the tendering of an offer for the assistant principalship. Leonard Pitts Jr. (2007) states it best: "What is at stake is the ability of people to trust that those in positions of trust are worthy of trust" (p. A9).

How is trust defined by the interviewer(s)? "People who *are* selected as administrators are likely to be those who are similar to previous administrators, people whose ways of thinking and acting coincide with tradition" (Marshall & Hooley, 2006, p. 15). This is usually referred to as the concept of *fit*. You will be wise to do your best to understand the culture of the school and school system to which you are applying in order to assess how you will fit and what wiggle room exists given your background, talents, and leadership style.

With all that said, there is another very important issue. It's a touchy subject. We all believe that we will prevail in the interview based solely on our intellect, ability to think on our feet, and overall leadership capacity. The truth is that you may be the best candidate for the job, but if your personal presentation communicates something in direct conflict with the district or superintendent, then that is a problem for you. Grooming and dress are critical in an interview. Don't forget it.

The best rule of thumb is not to do anything that will distract from your abilities or your vision. Perfume, overwhelming jewelry, loud-patterned clothing, unkempt hair, or even unruly whiskers can detract from the true purpose of the interview. Dress and groom appropriately. We are not trying to be condescending, but take note of how important this might be based on the following snapshot shared by an interviewer.

SNAPSHOT 5.2: I CAN'T GET PAST THIS

We looked at each other in disbelief. We could hardly keep it together. The candidate for the assistant principal vacancy looked great on paper. The credentials were amazing. References were good. Even the answers to the prepared questions were exactly what we wanted to hear. The only problem was that the candidate who sat in front of us looked like he had slept in his car.

As the interview progressed, we could not focus on what the man was saying. We were intent on his rumpled clothing and messed-up hair. How would students react to this person? How would parents relate? If we knew his resume and could not overcome his appearance, he would certainly have problems in our school district.

This potential candidate will not be hired. He may be an excellent assistant principal, but his appearance is overshadowing any credentials or abilities he may possess. Present yourself in a way that is true to yourself but also in line with what is considered professional in that particular school district. Do not underestimate the power of the first impression or, worse, the power of a *bad* first impression.

The process can be brutal. As perfect as you seem for the job, you might not be the candidate chosen. Don't give up and don't beat yourself up. Do evaluate each interview. Reflect on the questions that were asked and the responses you gave. Honestly assess how well you think you did. Make adjustments you need to make and move on. Each interview is an opportunity to grow.

In the next chapter we move to your first days on the job as an assistant principal. You now have the position and are able to shape it to the best of your ability. Your challenge will be to draw upon what you have learned as a teacher and graduate of a principal credentialing program to be a successful assistant principal.

QUESTIONS FOR DISCUSSION

1. Using a scale from 1 (low) to 5 (high), how do you assess your skills as a networker? (Note that we define "networking" as the developing of contacts and information.) Please give reasons and examples for your answer.
2. Using a scale from 1 (low) to 5 (high), how do you assess your skills as a networker with regard to employment opportunities? Give examples from past experiences.
3. What strategies do you have in mind for improving your networking skills with regard to employment as an assistant principal and/or principal?
4. Think for a few moments of persons you have known who have interviewed well for employment. What would you describe as the reasons for

their success? Are these reasons ones you presently employ? Are they ones you would be willing to try out?

5. What support system do you have in place that might be useful to you in successfully becoming an assistant principal? Are there any ways you could add to or improve this support system? Please be specific.

6. How can you find out what the school districts and schools you are interested in really believe and practice? Please give concrete examples.

7. How do you assess the concept of *fit* as described in this chapter? How does the concept apply to you, if at all, in pursuing an assistant principalship? Give examples, perhaps using "what if?" situations.

8. How do the epigraphs at the beginning of the chapter speak to you in your first steps in becoming a school administrator?

SUGGESTED READINGS

Bolman, L. G., & Deal, T. E. (2002). *Reframing the path to school leadership: A guide for teachers and principals.* Thousand Oaks, CA: Corwin Press.

Marshall, C., & Hooley, R. M. (2006). *The assistant principal: Leadership choices and Challenges* (2nd ed.). Thousand Oaks, CA: Corwin Press. See chapter 2, "How do assistant principals get their jobs?"

National Association of Secondary School Principals (NASSP). (2005). *Developing the 21st century school principal.* Reston, VA: NASSP.

First Days on the Job as an Assistant Principal

From the point of view of a superintendent or principal, it is critical that the assistant principal support the established routines and guide teachers in the established procedures. Clearly, assistant principals spend most of the early years in their role learning procedures and the school culture.

—*Catherine Marshall and Richard M. Hooley (2006, p. 15)*

The single most important factor in student achievement is the quality of the teacher.

—*Donna Foote (2008, p. 47)*

Principals do make a difference in school improvement and student achievement. As my colleague Kenneth Leithwood has concluded from his research, in impact on student learning, the principal is second only to the teacher.

—*Michael Fullan (2008, p. 36)*

Civility is hardly the only way to live, but it is the only way that is worthwhile.

—*M. Scott Peck (1993, p. 54)*

There is a tendency in our culture and society to discount entry-level jobs—the instructor at the university, the nurse and physician's assistant in the doctor's office, the recently hired attorney who is not a partner in the law firm, and the assistant principal in a school. In fact, there are those who believe that the most desirable quality in an assistant principal is to not attract attention.

The discounting of entry-level jobs in our culture and society is reflected in the fact that little attention in literature and scholarship has been given to the assistant principal, particularly in contrast to the amount of attention given to superintendents and principals (Marshall & Hooley, 2006). We have also discovered that most preservice programs in educational administration focus on the principalship, with scant attention given to the assistant principalship.

It is our view that this is a mistake, largely because it is the assistant principal who is in a position to make a significant difference in the lives of students, teachers, and others in our schools. The following snapshot makes this case.

SNAPSHOT 6.1: A CARING ASSISTANT PRINCIPAL REACHES A LONELY SIXTH GRADER

Carol is a sixth grader in a large middle school in a medium-sized city. It is the end of the first week of school in the fall and Carol stands in front of a fruit juice machine in the hall, looking forlorn and lost. Little wonder, as she no longer has the security of her elementary school and is just beginning a three-year career as a middle school student.

John Morris, an affable and gregarious assistant principal, approaches Carol and says, "I'm Mr. Morris. What happened to that second stretch thing that holds your hair together?"

Carol smiles and responds, "I lost it this morning."

"Here's what I'm going to do," John says. "I'm going to put money in this machine and you can choose any juice you want." He puts coins in the juice machine and Carol pushes the button of her choice. They talk for a few minutes, after which Carol walks into the cafeteria for lunch.

That night after school, when Carol is asked by her mother how school went that day, Carol smiles and tells her mother about Mr. Morris and what happened at the juice machine. When asked what Mr. Morris's job in the school is, Carol says, "I don't know. He's kind of a cool guy who works in the principal's office." Carol's mother finds out at a visit-the-school night that Mr. Morris is one of two assistant principals in the middle school.

This story has special meaning for me (Dale Brubaker) as Carol is my daughter, and I had a feeling of relief that she was beginning to feel at home in her new middle school after a few days of being lost. Her mother and I sensed that there was a caring person in a school leadership position who had the sensitivity to read Carol's needs and go out of his way to help meet them. Some people refer to such acts as "the power of one"—one caring person can make a difference in another person's life.

One of the interesting things about leadership in general and the assistant principalship in particular is that the leader can often work through his or her own challenges and needs by helping students and teachers who are also struggling in their own ways. This point was brought to our attention by what a school administrator told us.

SNAPSHOT 6.2: HELPING MYSELF BY HELPING OTHERS

My career as an educator may in some ways be considered charmed. That is, I was recognized for my abilities and things moved along quite smoothly. I'm not sure I ever really overcame the feeling, however, that I wasn't good enough or smart enough. As I look into the eyes of school administrators who have a depth of commitment to their schools, teachers, and communities and listen to them, I hear lamentations of what they've left behind, the sacrifice of family and relationships.

Hearing these stories during the first days of my assistant principalship, I wondered if the job would consume me. A number of questions entered my mind. Will my children simply include themselves among the hundreds of students in the school where I am an administrator? Will I primarily identify myself as a school administrator, not a woman, wife, mother, daughter, or sister? Will I use my work to justify everything from missed ball games to forgotten birthdays? Will I be able to find balance in my life?

A colleague who is an administrator assured me that there are ways to work toward such a balance. In fact, she advised me to write my commitments down and she would help hold me accountable for achieving such a balance. She added that the fullness of my leadership would be affected by how fully I experience the other roles in my life and it is in helping others that I will better understand myself, my challenges, and what it will take to live a balanced life. She helped me see that it was important for me to set standards early—standards that would help me work toward this goal of living a balanced life.

Our research on work-life balance indicates that achieving such a balance is one of the biggest challenges facing the school administrator (Coble, Clodfelter, & Brubaker, 2007, pp. 133–34). Respondents identified warning factors in the form of questions: Do you eat standing up so that you can get to work quicker? Do you interrupt others in order to close down the conversation to get back to your work? Do you multitask so much that you don't enjoy one thing at a time?

Respondents said that "audiotapes" frequently go off in their heads when they get to work: "I have to appear to be ambitious, intense, and driven to give the impression that I am a good leader." "I have to work all of the time to be acceptable." "I have to be working behind my desk to demonstrate that I am working hard." It was interesting to note that many school administrators felt they had to leave followers with the feeling that they, too, must always be working to be acceptable.

We identified a number of ways to help administrators deal with workaholism. We urged them to find ways to spend time with children in order to observe their awe, wonder, and amazement at the world around them. Leaders found that seeing a child's joy for living can be contagious. School administrators were also encouraged to make a list of ways to achieve a more balanced life.

They listed things like finding hobbies and events away from work that would take their minds off of work, sitting down with family and friends to identify things that are fun to do together, and finding informal organizations whose members are involved in interesting and fun activities. In seminars and workshops designed to achieve a better balance in life, leaders frequently referred to their operating style as "life on the run."

STEPPING INTO THE ROLE OF ASSISTANT PRINCIPAL

One of the first things you will notice in your first days as an assistant principal is how varied the role of the assistant principal is and therefore how diverse the expectations of others will be as you play this role. How can you sort out all of these expectations so that you can deal with them efficiently and effectively? Much of the sorting out will be done by the principal, the person who is officially recognized as the leader of the school. There is no single job description for the assistant principalship, and responsibilities and tasks are frequently assigned as needs emerge during the course of a school day.

The snapshots in this chapter will focus on some of the many task areas facing the assistant principal (Marshall & Hooley, 2006, pp. 5–7):

- Conferences with students, parents, and others
- Informal contact with students, teachers, and noncertified staff—for example, secretaries, cafeteria workers, and custodians

- Supervision of students as they get on and off buses and other transportation issues, such as guidelines for parents dropping off and picking up students at school
- Giving attention to personal growth and development—listening to evaluative comments by "bureaucratic superiors," teachers, parents, and others
- Improving curriculum and instruction—for example, improving high-stakes testing, inspiring and motivating teachers, evaluating teachers, working with teacher advisory committees, and improving in-service education for staff
- Handling behavior problems
- Public relations
- Working on the master schedule and other scheduling challenges
- Counseling students regarding educational programs and vocations
- Attendance
- Building maintenance
- Student activities
- Community activities
- Parking
- Conducting faculty meetings
- Lockers
- Textbook selection and allocation
- Scheduling of duties for teachers and others, for example, in the cafeteria and on the playground
- Rituals, such as graduation ceremonies
- Resolving disputes among employees and organizations

The list seems endless and the challenge of creating frameworks for dealing with such matters is an ongoing process. The epigraph by Catherine Marshall and Richard Hooley in this chapter is right on target.

Since the principal's leadership is a key factor as collaborative leadership between you and the principal develops, your assessment of the principal's primary interests, strengths, and challenges, as well as your own, is important. This is a part of what Marshall and Hooley (2006) call "role negotiation" (p. 123). Role negotiation recognizes the importance of autonomy in a professional's life and makes the case for not having too-tight role definitions for the assistant principal and principal. Trust between the assistant principal and the principal, as well as in the role negotiation process itself, is essential.

The way you use the following assessment instrument can be a sensitive matter, but nevertheless it is an indispensable first step in the collaborative leadership process for you to at least fill this out in your own mind. The following assessment form (figure 6.1) provides you with a framework for this assessment. You may complete this assessment alone and/or with the principal, depending on the relationship you have established. Please skip those items for which you presently have little, if any, information by which to make a judgment.

We hope you will be able to use this assessment instrument as a guide to discussing and sharing duties and responsibilities. It may also be useful to you

	Level of Competency			
	1 (low) to 5 (high)		1 (low) to 5 (high)	
Activities	P.	A.P.	P.	A.P.
1. Attention to large picture/framework	—	—	—	—
2. Attention to details	—	—	—	—
3. Public speaking (e.g., to PTA, civic clubs, faculty meetings, or graduations)	—	—	—	—
4. Informal conversations with parents, teachers, students, and others	—	—	—	—
5. Initiating projects	—	—	—	—
6. Maintaining projects	—	—	—	—
7. Completing projects	—	—	—	—
8. Dealing with student behavior problems	—	—	—	—
9. Dealing with teacher/staff problems	—	—	—	—
10. Curriculum, instruction/teacher assessment	—	—	—	—
11. Public relations	—	—	—	—
12. Delegation of assignments	—	—	—	—
13. Technological skills	—	—	—	—
14. Shared decision making	—	—	—	—
15. Professional development leadership	—	—	—	—

FIGURE 6.1
Assessment of Principal's and Assistant Principal's Interests, Strengths, and Challenges

if your interests move you toward a principalship in the near future. You will simply be in a different position in the role negotiation process.

PROBLEMS AND DILEMMAS

Given the list of activities you participate in as an assistant principal, you will probably be looking for sorting mechanisms that will help you group what you do in an efficient way. The first sorting mechanism we recommend is that of making a distinction between problems and dilemmas. For example, it is relatively easy for you as an assistant principal to answer a teacher's need for some instructional supplies, such as paper and pencils. This is a problem that can be solved.

It is, however, a dilemma that there will always be more demands than there are resources. You will not be able to answer all of the demands that make their way into your "in-box." This dilemma must simply be reconciled or lived with to the best of your ability. It can be useful to make lists of problems you can solve and dilemmas you must reconcile. The following snapshot serves as an example of a dilemma that an assistant principal faced.

SNAPSHOT 6.3: DEALING WITH MY PERFECTIONIST TENDENCIES

I have always been an excellent student who not only started tasks to be done but also completed them to the satisfaction of my teachers and professors. I was rewarded with good grades and academic honors.

One of my professors of educational administration said that as school administrators we should start with a clean desk in the morning and not leave at the end of the day without having a clean desk. During my internship I was somewhat aware of the workload awaiting me as an assistant principal, but it was as a beginning assistant principal that I began to realize that the more good work I did the more additional work would be piled on me.

I fell into the trap of being obsessed with completing my work perfectly. The more I fell into this trap, the more I turned to the problem as my solution. In other words, I simply worked harder and longer to get good strokes that made me feel better. As a result, I burned out even more.

I realized that I needed to learn to pace myself and find ways to deal with my perfectionism or I would be in real trouble. Fortunately, I respected the principal with whom I worked and felt that I could share this challenge with her. This was the beginning of a real attitude and behavior adjustment I needed to make.

School leaders with perfectionist tendencies were quite open and honest with us when we interviewed them as part of our research (Brubaker & Coble, 2007a). They said that they feared the loss of control and tried to alleviate this fear by trying to control everything around them.

One assistant principal said that her mentor, a principal, was a perfectionist who was used as an example of excellence by central administration. The principal arrived at school at least an hour before anyone else did. She checked on what custodians had done and would do any cleaning that was overlooked. She went from classroom to classroom to make them neater. She also did this in the cafeteria.

In fact, she was such an efficient micromanager that teacher leaders, some of whom were interested in becoming school administrators, didn't get any practice in leading in the school building. It was ironic that the principal, who talked a good deal about shared decision making, didn't seem to be aware that she was stealing from others opportunities to practice leadership.

It is important for you as an assistant principal to carefully observe the school to which you are assigned with regard to the leadership practiced by teachers and administrators. Decisions facing teachers are often dilemmas, the reconciliation of which is accompanied by pain. The following snapshot shows an example of a third-grade teacher who lost sleep and weight as she wrestled with a decision's implications for those influenced by what she would think and do.

SNAPSHOT 6.4: THE PRESSURE OF STANDARDIZED TESTING

Each school in our system has a report card that tells the public our annual goal, objectives, and plan of action. Our school's major goal was to raise standardized test scores. My class was moving along smoothly after a couple of weeks when a new student, a nonreader with low test scores, arrived on the scene from another town. My first reaction was "Why did I have to get this student? I wish he would move again!" At the same time I realized that I, a good teacher, was exactly the kind of person who could make a difference in his life.

We had a newly assigned principal in our school who I didn't know yet. I therefore decided to talk through this situation with our new assistant principal, who I knew and trusted as a former colleague and teacher.

If this teacher came to you with this dilemma, what advice would you give? Would you thank the teacher for candidly sharing the situation and the pain associated with it? Would you give the teacher a "sermon" on how all children's needs must be met? How would you reconcile the school's pressure on teachers to raise standardized test scores while at the same time honoring the preciousness of each child in the school? Would you involve the newly assigned principal in this matter? What experiences in your professional and personal life influenced your answers to the previous questions?

Your answers to these questions will begin to define your role as an assistant principal in the eyes of teachers and others in your school.

METAPHORS THAT REVEAL YOUR VIEW OF WHAT
SCHOOLS AND SCHOOLING SHOULD BE

Another thing to observe during your first days as an assistant principal is what metaphor(s) teachers, the principal, parents, and others use to describe the school. The most frequently used metaphor is that of the family: "We are a family here!" As M. Scott Peck (1993) has noted, the primary role of a family is to nurture its members. It is true that nurturing is a major role of effective principals and assistant principals.

Yet the family metaphor doesn't hold in other respects. Principals, often with the advice of assistant principals, hire and fire teachers and other staff members, for example. These functions are more accurately associated with a business or nonprofit organization rather than a family. In Robert Frost's poem, "The Death of the Hired Man," the husband, a farmer, says, "Home is where, when you have to go there, they have to take you in" (quoted in Peck, 1993, p. 196).

Another difficulty with the family metaphor for schools is that it is easy to conceive of schools as patriarchies or matriarchies, in which the principal, and perhaps the assistant principal, are benevolent and not-so-benevolent parents. Teachers and other staff members can, through transference, "a neurotic and uncivil distortion of reality," continue to relate to their new "father" or "mother" in positive or negative ways (Peck, 1993, p. 214).

In recent years, a more apt metaphor for a school is that of a business. Test scores and other number-related products are marketed by some teachers, principals, superintendents, and school board members. In fact, some superintendents refer to themselves as chief executive officers (CEOs). Parents and others are in turn referred to as clients.

At any rate, as an assistant principal, your use of a metaphor or metaphors to describe your school will tell others a good deal about the role you think assistant principals and principals should play. This issue is one that may be important to discuss in a faculty meeting and/or professional development setting.

The metaphor you use as an assistant principal to describe your school will be a distillation of your experiences as a K–12 student, a teacher, an undergraduate student, a graduate student in classes and the internship, and other events in your life. The following snapshot illustrates how an assistant principal reconciled the love of ideas with other matters during first days on the job.

SNAPSHOT 6.5: STRUGGLING TO KEEP MY LOVE OF IDEAS IN MY LEADERSHIP ROLE

I couldn't get an assistant principalship in the school or school system where I taught. I was lucky enough to have a friend from college get a principalship a hundred miles or so from my home, and he asked me in late July to be his assistant principal. Because this was a last-minute appointment, I decided to rent an apartment near my new school so that I wouldn't disrupt my family at the beginning of the school year. This would also give me a chance to see if I liked the job and school enough to stay. If not, I could try to return to a teaching position in the school where I was the year before.

I need to say something about my early experiences in formal education so that the issues I present will make sense. I grew up in a small town until the seventh grade. It was like a big family, with school and church a major part of my life. But, I also had a strong interest in sports—especially basketball, something I played in middle school and high school. In fact, the blue-collar city I moved to just before my seventh-grade year didn't have a strong college preparatory program in its high school. What little attention I gave to scholarship was because my mother, a teacher, insisted that I read and do as well as I could in school.

During my first two years of college, I took the basic required courses, continued to play basketball, and was an average student grade point–wise. The professor of English in the first course I took assigned a theme, and I handed in an outline instead. I didn't even know what a theme was.

The professor advised me to read, read, read. I asked him what to read. He responded, "At this point, anything will do!" The best thing one could say about my scholarship during the first two years of college was that I didn't burn out intellectually.

For some reason, I came to life during the first semester of my junior year in college. My courses were electives, and I fell in love with philosophy, history, and literature. I began to write and rewrite, finding it much like the piano and clarinet I played thanks to my mother's urging. To the great surprise of my college friends, my grade point average for the junior year was 4.0. As I look back on it, it is clear that it was during the junior year in college that I fell in love with ideas.

It is with this background in mind that I want to go back to the beginning days of my assistant principalship, when I returned each night to my apartment after long days at school. This was a place that gave me plenty of time to think about my new position and what I wanted to do with it.

I had several planning days with the principal before teachers came back to begin the school year. Fortunately, we had the kind of relationship where we could share our innermost thoughts and concerns. I told him about my love for ideas and how my graduate school education stimulated this interest.

I was part of a master's program that valued the life of the mind. Professors in the program brought in nationally known speakers each month. We read their articles and/or books before they lectured to us, followed by question-and-answer sessions. My favorite speaker was Lee Shulman, a professor at Stanford University. We read two of his articles that really spoke to me: "Teaching as Community Property" (1993) and "Appreciating Good Teaching" (an interview by Tell, 2001). I have a quote from him on the side of my file cabinet, where I can see it easily from my desk: "At the heart of my work on good teaching is the notion of a teacher as an enlightened, passionate intellectual."

My candid conversation with my friend, the principal, couldn't have been better. He explained that he saw his role as primarily being a good school manager. He added that he did recognize the importance of my interests in scholarship. He said that he would support me in any way possible. He added that a lot of parents in the community were professionals who were interested in their children's scholarship and he wanted their support.

I expected an uphill battle to further my interests, but I was happily surprised to discover the amount of support already in place in the school. When teachers returned to school, they brought me up-to-date on a faculty book club that met several times a year. It was also on the teacher leadership council's agenda to choose a book each year that would be read and discussed at faculty meetings at appropriate times. They wanted to use books by professors at nearby universities, if possible, with faculty and perhaps others attending meet-the-author sessions.

One teacher, who shared my interests and was obviously a leader on the faculty, probably gave me the best advice: "What is more important than anything else is the conversations you will initiate with faculty that demonstrate your love for ideas." I was reminded once again that leading by example is what really matters.

Reading this snapshot makes it clear that one of the metaphors this assistant principal had in mind for his school was that of a vibrant learning community, a community where the sharing of important ideas would be nourished (Noddings, 2007). (See appendix F, "Working Alone and Working in a Team.")

Given the assistant principal's love for ideas and his autobiography in relation to this commitment, we can expect some dissonance between his leadership in curriculum and instruction and the views of some others, including parents. For example, we have experienced more than a decade of emphasis in our schools on administrator accountability, which is taken to mean students doing well on high-stakes tests. The assistant principal is pressured on four levels: (1) national, (2) state, (3) district, and (4) the individual school. Although criticism of this emphasis and a highlighting of collateral damage has surfaced, the narrowing of educational goals and a shrinking curriculum continues (Thomas, 2005; Brubaker & Coble, 2007a).

How might this play out for the assistant principal in the previous snapshot and those of you who support the view that "the definition of a successful student has to change from one whose achievement is measured solely on the basis of test scores to one who is healthy, emotionally, and physically inspired, engaged in the arts, and prepared for employment in a global economy" (Honawar, 2007, p. 7)? (The question was raised in a report by the Association for Supervision and Development's Commission on the Whole Child.)

The case for a more encompassing definition of curriculum was made by James B. Macdonald (1977): "Curriculum is the environment in the school and in the classroom. You have there in miniature what you have in life outside of the classroom and the school. Curriculum is therefore life! That's why it is so vital and exciting. That's what makes it important. There's nothing out there that doesn't relate to curriculum."

Conversations we have had with school and school-system administrators, as well as teachers, lead us to believe that they acknowledge the importance of this wider view of curriculum while at the same time adding that they must take into account the political pressures associated with their jobs.

What you seek to accomplish in your new leadership role may be in conflict with what those around you perceive or their metaphor of what school should be. This may leave you wondering what impact you have as an assistant principal and how you can really affect the lives of students while considering the principal's, staff's, parents', and community's different ideas of what that should look like.

The politics, micro and macro, of what we do as leaders are often surprising, as the scrutiny we live under as teachers does not compare. Be prepared for what you did not expect when you set out to do your best. Hurtful and surprising sometimes, reactions of others deflate our enthusiasm. As an assistant principal wrestling with the issue of conflicting metaphors, remember the following as you begin your career.

1. *Everything you do sends a message.* Everything. Giving a teacher a different lunchtime than she has had for the past ten years sends a message that you obviously have it in for her. Fourth-period planning may be given to coaches to eliminate time away from classes due to early meets or matches, but it communicates that all you care about is football. If you answer your own calls, you don't have enough to do. If your secretary answers your calls, you are too good to pick up the phone. If you suspend a child for disrespect, you

are too hard and don't support children. If you don't suspend, then you are a pushover and don't support teachers. You will be criticized for the car you drive, the kind of clothes you wear, and how well you seem to "fit."

The long and short of it is that you will not win with everyone. There is power for positive and negative messages in every single decision you make. You will control some of these messages but have absolutely no control over others. It's just the nature of the job. While as a teacher you affected one set of parents and students, as an assistant principal you now affect many more.

Use the power of your decision making wisely. Try to think about what message you are sending through even managerial decisions like class scheduling and duty rosters. What you mean may not always be what is interpreted, but you can also send some positive messages through everyday decisions.

An assistant principal we know strategically chose students who were not involved in school clubs or sports to be responsible for raising the flag each day. Through this simple choice, he quietly communicated that we should reach out to involve all children in our schools in something.

Another assistant principal used the weekly newsletter to highlight teachers who were implementing the new reading strategy taught at the faculty meeting that week. She did not "hammer" those who were not embracing the new reading strategies, but chose to send a positive message about those who were on board.

2. *Every decision has a consequence you did not anticipate.* So you thought it all out and are sure you have anticipated all possible responses? No way! Even the best decisions will result in reactions you never would have imagined, as shown in the following incident shared by a new elementary assistant principal in a small, rural district.

SNAPSHOT 6.6: WHAT IS GOING ON HERE?

My principal and I decided that one of my major responsibilities would be to work with the PTA on fund-raising. We had a new guided-reading library we were trying to fill up with books and the PTA had designated a certain amount of fund-raising to go toward this project. I worked with the PTA executive board and we decided on a pizza night, when staff from the school would work in a local restaurant to prepare and serve food.

The restaurant owner had committed 30 percent of the sales from that evening to our PTA. The idea was that students would encourage parents to eat out at the pizza restaurant that night and boost our profits. We sent home flyers and made announcements at school, and the children seemed excited to come out and see their favorite assistant principal and teachers making and serving pizza.

What I did not anticipate was that someone could find fault with this activity. I could not believe it when the chairperson of the local chamber of commerce called me to chew me out for "favoring" a particular business in the community when so many others were struggling and could use the free advertisement we were giving the pizza place, which was not a member of the chamber of commerce.

Here I thought I was doing something good for our students, but now I was being chastised for not supporting community businesses. I had, with one decision, alienated businesses in my community. This was not my intent.

What happened to this assistant principal is not uncommon. We are often left thinking, "Did this really just happen?" What we say about this snapshot is to learn something. Attend the chamber of commerce meetings from now on. Rotate the fund-raiser restaurant from month to month. Establish relationships in the community that show you are supportive and appreciative of all its resources. Could you have anticipated this outcome? Maybe not, but you will next time.

3. *You did not sign up to be popular.* You know you are an administrator when the teachers stop talking when you walk into the lounge. It hurts a little

the first time, particularly if you have been colleagues. You will never get to tell your side of the story, because that would break confidentiality. Teachers, students, and parents will broadcast their sides of the story. They've already made up their own minds about what is true. Rarely will anyone rush to your defense.

SNAPSHOT 6.7: THE SURVEY

I decided early in my administrative assignment that I would not be one of those leaders who never asked for input. My idea was to collect information from stakeholders regularly via surveys, identify the areas of concern, and address them in a timely fashion, and to, by doing these things, be viewed as a responsive leader. The first surveys were a crushing blow. I cannot say I was not warned. My friend Gayle told me not to read them. I did not listen.

I had only asked a few questions: How is the schedule working for you so far? What is going well about your year? What could make your year better?

Two responses stood out. In the first response, the teacher disregarded the questions altogether and wrote "ON BACK" on the front of the survey. I turned it over, and she had written a diatribe about our recent half-day staff development. This particular date happened to be my birthday, and unbeknownst to me the staff members who were responsible for snacks that day provided a birthday cake with my name on it. The opening comment was, "We do not have time to celebrate Susie's birthday. Our time would have been better spent in our classrooms than singing 'Happy Birthday' to our assistant principal." She went on and on, but the opener sucked the wind out of me. Really? Did she not know that the district had mandated these days as professional development days? Did she not realize that we would have had snacks anyway and that I did not know that a birthday cake was being provided? Could I help being born on this day? Wow. I was stunned. I was hurt. I was not popular.

I should have stopped there but I decided to read on and was encouraged by some constructive feedback given about our new schedule and some positive comments about the start of our year. I should have quit when I was ahead. The final comment on the final survey was in response to the question, "What could make your year better?" The comment was "to have our old assistant principal back." I called my friend Gayle in tears. She told me to throw the surveys away.

This assistant principal actually continued to survey her staff. She shared all responses and proposed actions she would take to make things better and she moved on. The positive outcome is that after telling her to throw the surveys away, her friend Gayle focused her on the positive responses she received. When the assistant principal really considered the constructive feedback as compared to the toxic feedback, she realized that teachers who were truly concerned about making things better far outweighed those who were just trying to make her feel bad.

In the end, it does not matter if you are well-liked. What matters in the bottom line is that children's lives are made better by what you bring to the role.

4. *Leadership is lonely.* On the first workday when everyone is making lunch plans and you find yourself eating peanut butter and jelly alone at your desk, you begin to realize the magnitude of your solitude in this position. How could you possibly be in on the lunchtime banter when you are now "one of them"? Captured in the poignant reflections of a new high school assistant principal, lunch on workdays can be the most isolated time: "I always loved

Mexican on workdays. I loved going out with my friends and dishing about the administration, new teachers, or parents. It was great.

"Now that I am an assistant principal, no one invites me to lunch. I watch them go in groups. They walk right by but no one asks me to join in. For the first time in ten years, I did not eat out on the workdays. I ate alone."

5. *Schools exist for children—without them, schools would not exist.* No matter how misunderstood you might be as a leader, you are working for the children in your school, and that is powerful, meaningful work. We are all human and want to be liked, but as much as the opinions of the adults may matter, the education of the children matters more. Schools exist to serve children and to educate them. If every decision is for and about children, you will not go wrong. From deciding whether or not to have the traditional Halloween parade to holding teachers accountable for current curriculum, you are responsible for the children. All of them. All of the time.

FACING DIFFERENCES IN OUTLOOKS BETWEEN TEACHERS AND ADMINISTRATORS

One of the major issues facing you as an assistant principal is recognizing and dealing with the differing perceptions of teachers and administrators. Catherine Gewertz (2007) summarizes some of these differences based on a study of 4,700 teachers and 267 principals and assistant principals in 12 districts conducted by the Council of Urban Boards of Education, part of the National School Boards Association.

- Nearly all the administrators agreed that "students are capable of high achievement on standardized exams," but only three-quarters of the teachers concurred.
- Far more teachers than administrators said that students were not motivated to learn.
- Eighty-five percent of administrators disagreed with the statement that most students at their schools would not be successful at community college or a university; only 58 percent of teachers disagreed.
- Eighty-six percent of administrators said their teachers use good professional judgment; among the teacher respondents, 76 percent said administrators trust their professional judgment.

- Ninety-four percent of the administrators said they actively seek out opportunities for teachers to learn new instructional methods, while 78 percent of the teachers said they had sufficient opportunities of that kind (p. 5).

Nearly all of those who critiqued the discrepancy between teachers and administrators concluded that the more positive or optimistic views of administrators about students were due to the fact that they were not "in the trenches" with the students on a daily basis, as were teachers, who had a more realistic view (p. 5).

What then are the implications of this research for you as an assistant principal? First, although there are many things you can do to help teachers, acting as if you are still a teacher in the classroom on a daily basis is not one of them. Professors who claim that they are still K–12 administrators aren't being honest, and K–12 administrators who act as if they are still teachers "in the trenches" will also be misleading, if not dishonest. The differences in the roles of teacher and administrator don't have to be highlighted, but you, the assistant principal, do need to recognize and accept them.

Second, the fact that you *have been* a teacher can be a real plus in your relationship with teachers. Teachers will know because of your conversations with them that you can get behind their eyes to see and feel many of the things that they experience. At the same time, it is important that you recognize and can talk about the changes in the lives of teachers that have occurred since you were in the classroom, when it is appropriate to talk about such changes. This is also a matter of honesty and understanding.

Third, "All professionals want their lives to have . . . flexibility, support, opportunities for satisfaction and job enhancement, a degree of control over the way to carry out the work, ways to get a sense that their work makes a difference for children and, through them, for a better world" (Marshall & Hooley, 2006, p. 119).

There is one question that students ask teachers and teachers ask administrators: "Do you want to be here with me?" If, through your verbal and nonverbal behavior, you show that you do, you are using one of the most powerful sources of power available to you (Brubaker, 2004, p. 49). An educator was reminded of this one evening when his family went to a restaurant.

SNAPSHOT 6.8: THE POWER OF WANTING
TO BE THERE

We walked into the restaurant and the hostess greeted us cor-
dially, after which she led us to our table in an inviting setting.
Our server or waitperson approached our table and said, "Can
I help you?" in a voice devoid of emotion. She wasn't unpleas-
ant and she wasn't pleasant. She was simply there. Our family
reacted to her flattened affect by trying to pick up her spirits with
humor and caring comments. No response. The result of the lack
of interaction with her, the leader who was expected to set the
stage for a pleasant evening, was that the food was excellent but
the dining experience was not.

While riding home in the car, one of our children said, "She acted
as if she didn't want to be with us." A lightbulb went on in my
head: "I wonder how many times I have left people with that
impression when I was with them."

One of the most important things we have noticed in the relationship between
teachers and administrators is their attitudes and behaviors with respect to
hierarchies and shared decision making. You can walk into some schools and
there is clearly a command-compliance way of doing business. "I know where
I stand, what I need to do, and I do it," some teachers say. They may add,
"I'm not paid to make administrative decisions. My principal and assistant
principal are."

It may be implied by such remarks that the teacher is in charge in the
classroom and administrators need to recognize and respect this: "When the
door is closed, the students are mine." As one teacher remarked, "I have one
of the best classrooms in the school. It is farthest away from the principal's
office." The following snapshot illustrates a top-down, command-compliance
approach to leadership in a school.

SNAPSHOT 6.9: A PRINCIPAL "TALKS STRAIGHT" TO THE ASSISTANT PRINCIPAL

During the first week of school, the principal invited me to go out to dinner. He was known in the system as a veteran principal who knew his way around the system. He got most of what he wanted because, in his own words, "I know where the bodies around here are buried." He was personable and you sensed that he was in charge. As we sat in the restaurant booth, he said he wanted to give me, his newly appointed assistant principal, "straight talk" about his expectations. This is what he said.

"It is easy to talk about teacher leadership and shared decision making but the principal is responsible for what happens in the school. We can talk all we want about flattening the organization, shared decision making, and stuff like that as alternatives to top-down traditional management systems, but we can't eliminate the fact that one person is officially appointed to accept ultimate responsibility for what goes on in the school as a whole. That person is the principal. The buck stops with me. If the school goes off track, I'm the one who is called into the superintendent's office. That's the way the teachers like it. They don't have to be responsible if something goes wrong in the school. They know it is my job to be the 'flak catcher when central office gets upset. I tell them that. In fact I have a fake hand grenade on my desk and I tell my teachers that when it goes off I will take the hit for them."

To be honest with you, I had mixed feelings about his straight talk. Part of me appreciated his strength, conviction, and honesty in telling me where he stood. It was like the feeling I had when my father told me that he would take care of me. I also knew that if I followed his orders and did a good job I would be taken care of—even with good job offers as a principal or central office supervisor in time.

But another part of me raised several questions: "How am I going to gain confidence as a leader in my own right if I simply obey his commands and don't get the practice I will need to be a leader who values shared decision making? Why do his tone and demeanor leave me with the feeling that I am weak and he is strong? And how can I serve as a leader who values shared decision making with teachers if I don't model this leadership? How much wiggle room will I have given his views?"

What are your options as an assistant principal in this case? You can openly voice your questions knowing full well that you may risk your working relationship with the principal, given his views and demeanor. You can thank him for sharing his views with you and go your own way at the school, knowing that you will have bumps in the road when problems arise. You can thank him for sharing his views, learn all you can as a new assistant principal, use what wiggle room you have, if any, and bide your time until a new job opportunity arises. Are there any other options that you have in mind?

In spite of the principal's demeanor in the previous snapshot, it is true that the principal does have positional authority as the officially appointed head of the school as an organization. However, if the principal is committed to giving you, the assistant principal, and teacher leaders opportunities to lead, all of you can profit from this experience.

You will be able to use your communication skills, listening and speaking, in order to develop expertise, an important source of power as a leader. (See appendix O, "Sources of Power Available to You as an Educational Leader and Decision Maker.") You will also be able to draw from your charisma and succor, a kind of counseling, to lead teachers, parents, and others in your school. (See appendix P, "Some Thoughts on Professional Development Leadership.")

One of the greatest satisfactions we have as university professors is observing you as assistant principals hone your leadership skills in working with teachers and others in advisory committee settings. It is in these settings and informal situations throughout the school that you use your talents to help others identify and use their talents—our definition of creative leadership (Brubaker, 2004). The following snapshot speaks to this matter.

SNAPSHOT 6.10: THREE INCIDENTS REACH THE PRINCIPAL'S ADVISORY COUNCIL

The first incident occurred in December, a month fraught with difficulties due to the pressures teachers and administrators have at home in the holiday season. The issue concerned the location of the teacher assistants' workroom in the school. At the beginning of our move to shared decision making in the school, the assistants were moved from the stage in the cafeteria to an area in the multipurpose room. This area was partitioned by bulletin boards and wasn't the least bit soundproof.

Because the physical education teacher and others used the multipurpose room for their activities, it was difficult for assistants to do work that required concentration, and the noise that assistants made working machines disturbed classes held in the multipurpose room. As the cold weather approached, the problem was accentuated, because more physical education classes had to be held inside the school. This raised the question in the advisory council, "How can teacher assistants be afforded the dignity and fair treatment given to teachers?"

The second issue concerned the supervision of children on the playground during recess time. Some staff members simply weren't supervising students well, with the result being fights and injuries to students. The dilemma can also be raised in the form of a question: "How can students receive adequate supervision from some teachers and assistants so that other teachers can have time away from the children during recess time?"

The cafeteria was the location of the third issue. Once again, some teachers and assistants didn't provide adequate supervision of students. When a cafeteria gets out of hand, the noise level is intolerable, food and other objects are thrown, and pushing, shoving, and fighting occur. The same question could be raised about the cafeteria that was raised about the playground: "How can students receive adequate supervision from some teachers and assistants so that other teachers can have time away from children during lunchtime?"

Advisory council members met with the teachers they represented and brought their recommendations back to the advisory council. All of these issues were dilemmas that involved resource allocation. A meeting with the principal was held and decisions, treated as proximate rather than fixed, were made by the principal. The assistants used the faculty lounge for their work and teachers assumed more responsibility on the playground and in the cafeteria. Not everyone was completely satisfied, but teachers and assistants were treated as professionals whose voices were heard. A new kind of culture began to emerge among teachers, staff, and the school itself.

A high school in the same school system provides us with another example of how assistant principals and principals had an opportunity to use their informal sources of collaborative power to influence decision making in the areas of curriculum and instruction. You will note in this snapshot that assistant principals, teachers, and others can often have indirect influence on principals, superintendents, and central office leaders. As someone once said, "You can accomplish anything if you don't have to receive credit for it."

SNAPSHOT 6.11: BRINGING HELPFUL CONSULTANTS INTO OUR SCHOOL

Our superintendent of schools prides himself on his interest in and leadership on behalf of curriculum and instruction. As a result, he and his wife, who works for the state Department of Instruction, make frequent trips to conventions featuring innovative programs and projects.

Central office consultants in our school system, in areas such as math, science, social studies, and language arts, use their networks of contacts in the school system, including assistant principals and principals, to gather the most recent literature on curriculum innovations and deliver this, along with convention advertisements, to the superintendent. Sometimes they deliver it in person to make their sales pitch. And it works!

Our arts program, for example, had tremendous human and nonhuman resources given to it after our superintendent went to a convention and heard a speech on connoisseurship by Eliot Eisner of Stanford University. Eisner was brought in as a consultant, and we used many of his materials. The arts are usually the first to be cut in this age of accountability and high-stakes testing, and our superintendent's interest in Eisner's work made a very positive difference in our school system.

As a proactive assistant principal, you can list the speakers and other consultants you were introduced to in your principal certification program. You can add to this list people you have heard at conferences and conventions. You can then use your network of contacts to influence the people in your school system who can bring to your school consultants who can make a positive difference for teachers, staff, parents, and students. Many of these people may already be in your community or vicinity and some of these people will even come to your school pro bono—*free*! (See appendix K, "What Works and Doesn't Work in Doing Professional Development.")

As you do more and more with shared decision making, you will hone your skills as a speaker, moderator, and disseminator of information. Progress reports, newsletters, news releases, radio and television interviews, and other accounts of events at your school can be powerful ways to bring attention to good things going on in your school. See appendix M, "How Good (and Comfortable) Are You as a Public Speaker and Listener?" and appendix N, "Guidelines for Going on Television." In some cases, you will be introducing the public to educational reform efforts. (See appendix L, "Preparing to Give Leadership to Educational Reform Efforts.")

PUBLIC RELATIONS: THE CIVILITIES OF LEADERSHIP

As an assistant principal, you will be one of the first persons the public meet when they enter the school. It is useful to remember one of the adages in the luxury hotel business: "If you manage the first and last impressions of a guest properly, then you'll have a happy guest" (Kleinfield, 1989, p. 36). Deborah Kenny, founder of Harlem Village Academies, caught the spirit of the luxury hotel metaphor: "We pay as much attention to parents and pay them as much respect as Ritz-Carlton workers are trained to treat their guests" (Lowry, 2008, p. 2). You and the principal will also have the opportunity to create a setting that will welcome parents, teachers, and others. The two snapshots that follow will demonstrate how different a setting can be (Brubaker, 2006, pp. 8–9).

SNAPSHOT 6.12: MY FIRST ENCOUNTER IN MY CHILD'S SCHOOL

It was a beautiful spring day when I first approached the school. I immediately noticed how well-kept the school's grounds were. I could smell the wild onions from the first grass cutting of the year and there were beds of spring flowers just beginning to bloom. As I approached the main entrance, I saw an attractive sign with a greeting in English and Spanish.

As I entered the main office, I saw a small group of adults, teachers, and assistants gathered around the secretary's desk. I stood there for several minutes watching the secretary sell clothes and beauty products (what I later learned was a side business, with most of her products displayed in the teachers' lounge).

When the secretary approached me, there was no greeting of any kind, simply a quizzical, "Yes?" I explained that I needed information on this particular magnet school and was surprised when she did not give me any written information on the school. In fact, I was left with the feeling that the secretary didn't want her world interrupted. I also noticed she had poor English: "The assistant principal usually don't come in this early as she is out with the buses."

SNAPSHOT 6.13: MY SECOND ENCOUNTER IN THE SCHOOL

My child didn't get into our first choice of magnet schools, and so I returned to this school once again, a school with a math/science emphasis. The flowers I saw earlier in the spring were now in full bloom and the school grounds were immaculate.

I was surprised on entering the front office to be greeted by a newly hired secretary: "Good morning! Welcome to our school. I'm Miss Bradburn, the school secretary. How may I help you?"

She had a warm smile on her face and gave me her full attention. Miss Bradburn then turned to her well-organized file cabinet, gave me some photocopied handouts, and told me what I needed to do in order to register my child. I immediately noticed Miss Bradburn's professionalism and good English—in contrast to the earlier secretary.

Miss Bradburn left me with the impression that she enjoyed her job, had pride in the school, and found my child and me to be special people deserving of attention.

Since both of the snapshots you have just read were located in the same school or physical setting, we can see that the school grounds were a real plus, for they sent the message that administrators cared enough about this school and its occupants to have inviting lawns and flowers as well as a well-kept building exterior. Furthermore, the welcome signs in both English and Spanish demonstrated inclusion.

The secretary in the first snapshot had a conflict of interest or divided loyalty between her work at school and her private business. She set the stage for the visiting person with mixed signals, thus conveying the message that the core values of the school itself were ambiguous. In fact, teachers were so used to the secretary's behavior that they hardly noticed it. They liked her personally and overlooked her flaws. The immediate question that comes to mind is, "Why did the administration of the school allow this to happen?" When this snapshot is brought to the attention of principals in leadership seminars across the nation, the following is a summary of their reactions.

Some school systems have policies that clearly state that school employees can't engage in such sales practices. Others don't. The enforcement of such policies in schools depends on the administration of the schools that have them and those in central office who supervise administrators in the schools.

Unfortunately, the secretary, in part because of her divided interests, was not well organized and didn't have the printed information requested by the visitor. Her poor English was an inadvertent misrepresentation of educational professionalism. She was what Erving Goffman (1959) calls a performance risk.

The second secretary used a number of inviting *civilities of leadership* to convey a positive invitation to the school, its magnet program, and the educators in the school. By giving her timely, complete, and undivided attention to the visitor interested in this magnet school, Miss Bradburn exhibited special attention-giving behavior to the visitor, thus leaving the visitor with the feeling that she and her child were important—the ultimate compliment to any person.

It is worth noting with regard to entrance rituals that one of the first things hotel workers are told is that eye contact is a necessary behavior for greeting guests when they arrive at the hotel (Kleinfield, 1989). Such contact communicates your willingness to go out of your way to help persons entering the setting, and it says you are risking a certain kind of vulnerability on their behalf.

It has always been interesting to us to watch some leaders use smiles and other nonverbal behaviors to relax persons entering a setting. They also exhibit the ability to establish a connection with so-called small talk. Leaders who are sensitive to entrance rituals quickly read a situation and go the extra mile to help others.

Leaders who give attention to entrance rituals know the importance of the physical setting. For example, one school principal inherited a high counter that served as a barrier between guests and the secretary. The counter was removed to facilitate exchange of ideas and feelings. Another principal instructed secretaries and student assistants to begin conversations with guests by saying, "Welcome to *our* school. How may I help you?"

A good energy level on the part of the greeter is important, but it is not sufficient in itself. Guests want to know that school leaders have a sense of purpose so that students, teachers, and others are involved in meaningful activity. A clear and concise vision statement communicates this sense of direction: "Everything we do here is aimed at helping students and adults become the best they can be." This general vision statement can be followed by more specific goals for the school. These statements are of little value if their owners can't share them with visitors in their conversations during normal school activity—for example, while walking down the hall of the school.

Our discussion of entrance rituals, one example of the civilities of leadership, has centered on the decorum of the school. It is fascinating to simply sit in a chair in the school office and listen to the ways in which adults relate to each other and the students. It is in such situations that the unobtrusive guest hears comments that reflect on what Goffman (1959) refers to as treatment of the absent. Teachers and secretaries will make comments about colleagues and students who are not within earshot.

Exit rituals are as important as entrance rituals. (It is worth noting that many religious services have both a processional and recessional—the entrance of the choir and clerics and their exit.) A major purpose of the exit ritual is to leave the participants, especially visitors, with the feeling that what they have experienced is worthwhile.

You, the assistant principal, by walking parents and others to the door, have the opportunity to prolong your conversation and demonstrate your care. It is an opportunity to summarize what has happened during the visit, thank them for their interest in students and the school, and invite them back for another visit.

It is during exit rituals that you will be reminded that "there is no more loyal guest than one who has a problem that gets fixed" (Kleinfield, 1989, p. 32). Luxury hotel surveys have also revealed time and again "that guests very much like being called by name" (Kleinfield, 1989, p. 35). A certain distanced respect is usually communicated by using "Mr." and "Ms.," unless the host is on a first-name basis with the guest.

With regard to exit rituals, it is also important to remember that the way you, the assistant principal, leave is often the way you will be remembered. A recent experience in hearing two university presidents speak on the same afternoon at the same site—a university auditorium—made this clear.

The first president gave a fine speech based on his knowledge of philosophical issues as applied to everyday challenges in higher education. The second speaker gave an acceptable, but not outstanding, speech delivered in a personable and caring manner. The two speakers left the speakers' platform at the same time. The first speaker hurriedly moved down the aisle without acknowledging persons on either side of the aisle. The second speaker spent a half hour or so talking to, listening to, and sharing his warmth with interested persons on both sides of the aisle.

It was surprising at the luncheon that followed when conversation after conversation centered on the warm and caring leadership of the second speaker. The first speaker's love for ideas was no substitute for a caring exit ritual.

Listening can be one of the most important civilities of leadership that you can practice as an assistant principal. The two snapshots that follow will take you into the lives of two assistant principals, one who is a poor listener and one who is a good listener. You see from these snapshots how important listening can be in establishing your credibility as an assistant principal. Snapshot 6.14 portrays a distracted assistant principal who is a poor listener. Snapshot 6.15 introduces us to a principal whose true listening is a real source of power.

SNAPSHOT 6.14: PORTRAIT OF A
HIGH FLIER

Jim was identified as a "high flier" from the time he began teaching. He knew how to get and keep the attention of his principal, central office leaders, the superintendent, and even the board of education. When he introduced new ways of teaching, he had press and television coverage. He was a real networker and had university professors invite him into teacher education classes to describe his innovative teaching practices. He became known by his colleagues as a "lone ranger" who had all the moves to get ahead in his career. He was definitely going places in a hurry, thus giving him "high flier" status.

Jim cultivated a good relationship with his principal and was asked to serve in the principal's role when the principal left the school for meetings and the like. Jim quickly went through the educational leadership program in a nearby university and was named assistant principal in the same system where he taught.

The one problem that many educators in the system associated with Jim was his poor listening. If you were talking with him in a public setting, such as a conference for principals and assistant principals, Jim was always looking over your shoulder to see if he should be talking with someone else—a person with more power and higher status. It was really quite embarrassing, for Jim would abruptly end the conversation with you and bolt toward the more important person. The interesting thing is that nobody brought this listening problem to Jim's attention as a graduate student or assistant principal.

SNAPSHOT 6.15: PORTRAIT OF A TRUE LISTENER

Dwight was an articulate, well-dressed assistant principal who was liked by everyone. He was one of the most personable and social persons in the school system.

Somewhere along the line, Dwight had learned the value of true listening. When you talked to him, you had the feeling that he genuinely cared about what you had to say. He gave you his undivided attention. When administrators in the urban school system met with spouses or friends at social gatherings, Dwight always seemed to be in the middle of the action—listening and rarely talking.

When Dwight walked down the hall of his school, teachers, their assistants, and students would suddenly appear in order to talk to Dwight. He always seemed to have time to meet with them.

One of the interesting things about Dwight was that he didn't send signals that he wanted to compete with other assistant principals. He had the ability to quickly and unobtrusively blend into situations and groups. As a result, he was known as a team player who people enjoyed working with on committees and projects.

Whether Dwight knew it or not, he sent the message to those talking that he was eager to learn more about them and what they had to say. It is simply flattering to you as a speaker when someone is a good listener, and it demonstrates that the listener isn't self-centered.

By actively listening you will communicate that you understand where the speaker is coming from, and that you care enough about that person to step into his or her shoes. Make no mistake about it, listening is hard work—what M. Scott Peck has called a manifestation of love (Peck, 1978). It relies on the discipline of bracketing, "the temporary giving up or setting aside of one's own prejudices, frames of reference, and desires" (Peck, 1978, p. 128).

The true listener temporarily communicates total acceptance of the speaker, the result being that the person speaking will feel less threatened and will make himself or herself more vulnerable by telling you more. Richard Amme (2003), media consultant, also reminds us that focusing our attention, a key to good listening, can be achieved by leaning forward and looking directly into the eyes of the person talking. This will keep your mind from wandering and encourage the speaker to say more.

One of the driving forces that can help each of us become true listeners is our desire to learn more about the person speaking and the subject of the conversation. The good listener, therefore, often stimulates conversation by asking a good question.

Goffman (1959) believes that a member of a team uses listening as a way to help others see that cooperation is essential and that the task to be performed is more important than meeting the ego needs of any one person.

Jim's narcissism and intense drive for a higher position, as described in snapshot 6.14, may well lead to political payoff but at a price to others and himself: "Politicians strike me as a lonely crowd, making few deep friendships because almost every relationship is tainted by the calculus of power: How will this help me?" (Smith, 1988, p. 92). Dwight, on the other hand, may well achieve a higher position but at a slower rate. Our guess is that he will enjoy the journey more and find the love of learning a lifelong benefit.

A superintendent of schools had a special interest in helping beginning assistant principals find their way in school administration. He shared the following with an orientation session in the fall of the year: "Administrators are overwhelmed with busyness. Most people want to climb the ladder of success in administration only to find that they constantly raise the ladder. When you get in the higher positions, you realize that large institutions are never picnics. They are like the ants without the picnics. People constantly harass you with problems that consume your resources."

In conclusion, simple kindnesses or civilities can make a real difference as assistant principals work with principals, teacher leaders, and others to create learning settings that will benefit students and themselves. The biggest enemy of many educational leaders is their constant need to be the center of attention in order to have their egos fed.

A colleague, coauthor, and friend, Larry Coble, cited former University of North Carolina president William Friday as an example of a leader who honored the civilities of leadership. Friday, although incredibly smooth, has an uncanny ability to shift the focal point of attention to the other person(s) when he interacts. He never fails to show his genuine interest and concern through his interpersonal skills, while many other leaders project themselves as know-it-alls.

We encourage you to add to our discussion of the civilities of leadership by describing those times in your life when others used their seemingly small acts of kindness to enrich your personal and professional life. You may then identify ways in which you can pass on these civilities in your role as an assistant principal.

CREATING A CULTURE OF LEADERSHIP THAT DEALS WITH STRESS IN A POSITIVE WAY

We conclude this section of the chapter on stepping into the role of the assistant principal by discussing a subject that assistant principals bring to our attention repeatedly: dealing with stress—the stress of the assistant principalship and therefore the stress of those influenced by the assistant principal.

The challenge is best framed in the form of a question: What can the assistant principal do to help create a culture that deals with stress in a positive way? We begin by recognizing that stress is inevitable in human interaction. To deny this is to give away the credibility you have as a leader. Those being led would recognize in such denial that you are out of touch with the reality of their professional lives.

Stress is primarily caused by the fear of being out of control. Anger and anxiety often go hand in hand with this fear. Depression, sometimes of a spiraling kind, may also be part of the equation.

What options do you as an assistant principal have in dealing with your own stress as it influences the leadership culture of the school and therefore the way those you lead relate to their stress?

First, you can sometimes eliminate or certainly minimize sources of stress. An example follows.

SNAPSHOT 6.16: THE SECRETARY AND THE SUPPLY ROOM

It was certainly going to be an interesting year at school. The principal and I were newly appointed, and we inherited a secretary who pretty much ran the school. The principal and I got an earful at our first teachers' advisory council meeting. The secretary was consistently criticized for tightly controlling the instructional supply room. When teachers wanted supplies, they had to go to the secretary "hat in hand" to ask for pencils, for example, after which the secretary unlocked the supply-room door and got the exact number of pencils she thought appropriate to meet your request.

The principal and I were committed to creating a new school culture that treated teachers as professionals, and we knew that the anger and stress behind the criticism of the secretary's tightfisted practices needed to be addressed in order to increase the morale of the faculty. The principal and I knew that our addressing this issue would be symbolic *and* real.

The principal talked to the secretary and informed her of the new policy that would be in effect. That same afternoon, he talked to the faculty at their orientation meeting and announced the new supply-room policy. The principal said that faculty members were to use their professional discretion in getting supplies from the supply room. Smiles of approval were on the faces of teachers in hearing the news.

The principal and I knew that this was the first of several issues that needed to be addressed with the secretary. As I said to him, "There's a new sheriff in town!"

A middle school principal in Portland, Oregon, had an interesting response to this snapshot. He advises us that the way the principal handled this case may mislead you as leaders to think you can set up situations that will create "train wrecks." This secretary probably has a power base within the building that is long-standing and potentially toxic.

Also, she has probably been managing the budget and knows what the school can and cannot afford. So, while teachers may be happy with what the principal did in the snapshot, this other realm may make so much trouble that the approach could cause a train wreck.

Administrators have to choose their battles and choose them carefully. Train wrecks cause huge stress for administrators. In the supply-closet snapshot, there is an alternative way of proceeding, based on talking to the secretary, finding out her concerns, and then working to come to a happy medium.

Another example of stress caused by noninstructional staff came to our attention in a small-town high school where the head of the cafeteria had ruled with an iron fist for years.

SNAPSHOT 6.17: THE HOTDOG PROBLEM

Mrs. Anderson had been head of the cafeteria for more than forty years and was known for her unconventional and sometimes unpredictable practices of keeping high school students in line in our small town. She was the topic of conversations at reunions when graduates discussed characters they had experienced at the high school.

It wasn't that Mrs. Anderson broke school rules. She didn't even know the school rules since the only rules she followed were her own—usually made up on an ad hoc basis, when the occasion arose. It was during one of her "spells," as they were called, that she crossed the line and became the talk of the school.

Mrs. Anderson hated wasting food, and it never happened if she could avoid it. One way it was avoided was for her and her staff to take home any "extra" food at the end of the lunch hour. Another way was for her to give lectures to students who didn't eat all of their food during lunch. She also wouldn't give students any extra food they requested, although she provided this service for maintenance workers in the school system who dropped by for her respected cooking. "Big hard-working men need a lot to eat," she would say.

One day she discovered that some girls who didn't like their hotdogs took them anyway and gave them to their hungry boyfriends in the lunchroom. Mrs. Anderson strode into the lunchroom, grabbed a hotdog from a boy's mouth, and said "This won't happen in my cafeteria!" She threw what remained of the hot dog in the garbage can and angrily strode back to her place behind the serving counter.

As you might imagine, Mrs. Anderson's act was the talk of the school for the day. Some teachers were particularly disturbed by her behavior but were reluctant to do anything given the ability of Mrs. Anderson to spread rumors and criticize teachers she disliked. The principal and I discussed the matter, after which the principal told her that her behavior was totally unacceptable. The principal said that she had a sullen look on her face but said nothing. (She retired later that year.)

The principal who spoke of "train wrecks" in reacting to snapshot 6.16 made an interesting observation with regard to snapshot 6.17. He advises us that after a person gets a job as assistant principal, the odds are pretty good that the assistant principal will be starting in the summer, with exposure only to the principal, secretary or secretaries, custodians, and other district employees. He adds that this time before the academic year begins can be used to get a real grip on the organization.

As might be expected, some of the stress assistant principals experience is the result of difficult relationships with teachers. You will note that it is always wise to keep an eye on how other teachers and staff members react to the ways in which you address these difficult relationships. The total culture of the school is influenced by your decisions. This is demonstrated in the following snapshot.

SNAPSHOT 6.18: RELIGIOUS PRACTICES AND THE SCHOOL

A number of changes took place when the school year began in our middle school. The city school system merged with a nearby rural system in which our middle school is located. Both the principal and I, the assistant principal, were new to the school.

Teachers returned to the school a week before students arrived. Their first priority was the arrangement of their classrooms. Classrooms came to life as bulletin boards were decorated and desks, chairs, and furniture were placed where teachers wanted them.

A new social studies/language arts teacher came to my office with a concerned look on her face. She said that a member of her teaching team, a veteran teacher, had a table next to the wall in her room with religious symbols on a long, white strip of cloth on the table.

I thanked her for her input and talked to the principal about this matter later in the day. Although I am a minister's daughter and member of the same denomination as the teacher, I knew she was in hot water. I was stressed out about how this might play out in the school, the newly merged school system, and the larger community—especially if it hit the newspaper and television stations.

The newly appointed principal talked to the veteran teacher who said she had simply lived her religion by having these symbols in her classroom and this was the first time in her many years of teaching in the school system that anyone had complained. She was distraught and reluctantly removed the religious symbols from her classroom.

At the end of the second week of school, the principal received a strongly worded letter of complaint from a parent, a journalist at the city newspaper, who said that his family had recently moved into the area. He said that his son's social studies teacher had posted religious articles on her bulletin board and was proselytizing in class.

The principal spoke to the veteran teacher, the same one he had admonished earlier, and she removed the articles from the bulletin board and announced she was retiring in December. There was some talk about this in the school and a lot of talk about it in the rural community, but I was relieved that this situation didn't "blow up" in the city newspaper and on television.

This snapshot reinforces the point that religion and politics are subjects that can be very controversial. Your background in school law may be especially useful in dealing with such matters. Other administrators in your school and/or school system may also be especially helpful as reactors to problems you face and as members of a core group that supports you emotionally and with knowledge.

A second way you can deal with stress in the assistant principalship is to change your own thinking. You can reframe the way you look at things. A simple example of this took place one Monday morning when an assistant principal walked through the side door of the principal's office rather than the front door that people normally used. The assistant principal said to the principal, "You've rearranged your furniture!" The principal responded with a smile on his face, "No, you just came through a different door to my office."

Distortions in our thinking may occur as we listen and interpret what we hear and don't hear. The secret is to identify these distortions so that we reframe them and don't act them out. David Burns (1980), author of *Feeling Good*, has identified ten cognitive distortions, with some overlap among them (Brubaker, 2006, pp. 15–17).

1. *All-or-nothing thinking* refers to your "tendency to evaluate your personal qualities in extreme, black-or-white categories" (Burns, 1980, p. 31). An assistant principal who was a disappointed candidate for a principalship demonstrated this cognitive fallacy: "Because I didn't get the principalship, I know I just don't have what it takes." An assistant principal who approached a health club about discounted memberships for interested faculty members received a positive response from the health club if at least ten teachers signed up for membership. There was great faculty interest at

a faculty meeting. However, only three teachers signed up for membership. The assistant principal was disheartened and said to a friend, "This is the last time I'm going to initiate anything like this!"

2. *Overgeneralization* is to "arbitrarily conclude that one thing that happened to you once will occur over and over again" (Burns, 1980, p. 32). A newly appointed assistant principal shared her disappointment in leading her first seminar at a nearby university: "This is the first and last time I am going to teach university students. I was a good university student, but I am no professor." Another assistant principal, disappointed with his lack of teaming with the principal, remarked, "This is the last time I am going to serve as an assistant principal in this school system."

3. A *mental filter* is in place when "you pick out a negative detail in any situation and dwell on it exclusively, thus perceiving that the whole situation is negative" (Burns, 1980, p. 33). An assistant principal said, "We have a lot of left-brained people on our faculty. The one time I tried a more right-brained approach to professional development, it didn't work. Teachers wanted lists and sequential professional development materials at the expense of looking at the total picture and being creative. I don't want to take a chance on using a right-brained approach to professional development again." Another assistant principal described a PTA meeting as follows: "I gave such a poor introduction of the principal to parents that the whole program simply fell flat."

4. *Disqualifying the positive* takes place when "you don't just ignore positive experiences, you cleverly and swiftly turn them into their nightmarish opposite" (Burns, 1980, p. 34). An assistant principal said to a parent, "Thanks for the compliment about my leadership, but you're just being nice." Why do we disqualify the positive? An assistant principal said, "I'm just beating my critics to the punch." There is a tinge of paranoia in the comment.

5. *Jumping to conclusions* exists when "you automatically jump to a conclusion that is not justified by the facts of the situation" (Burns, 1980, p. 35). This is a kind of *mind reading* because "you make the assumption that other people are looking down on you and you're so convinced about this that you don't even bother to check it out" (Burns, 1980, p. 35). An assistant principal said, "I know that our school can't implement this new, broader definition of 'curriculum' because the faculty simply won't buy

it." Another assistant principal told a friend, "I know that the open supply room idea won't work because a few hoarders will steal us blind."

6. *Magnification and minimization* occur when "you are either blowing things up out of proportion or shrinking them" (Burns, 1980, p. 36). "If our faculty sends this e-mail to the superintendent," an assistant principal said, "she will think the principal and I are terrible administrators." This magnification states an extreme case. It is similar to extreme minimization, on the other end of the spectrum, as follows: "The superintendent won't even notice this e-mail from the faculty, she is so busy."

7. *Emotional reasoning* exists when "you take emotions as evidence of the truth" (Burns, 1980, p. 37). "I really feel guilty about not being a curriculum leader," an assistant principal said. He added, "I know teachers expect me to be more involved in curriculum and instruction." One problem with this cognitive distortion is that you don't just get on with being a curriculum leader but instead wallow in the guilt.

8. *Should statements* are an attempt to "try to motivate yourself by saying, 'I should do this or that'" (Burns, 1980, p. 38). "I should be a better speaker at parent-teacher meetings" serves as an example. "I should do more reading in order to be up on what is going on in the leadership literature" is another example. These statements once again lead to one's simply being stuck in guilt. Your resources are misplaced when this happens. You don't move ahead with your stated intention.

9. *Labeling and mislabeling* create "a completely negative self-image based on your errors" (Burns, 1980, p. 38). We have often heard school and school-system administrators say, "I never have been *a scholar*. I'm an administrator—*a people person*." This kind of cognitive distortion narrowly defines the role of the scholar. "He and his brother both went to a *second-rate* university and became *second-rate* teachers," a critic said. "Of course she's bright," the critic added. "She went to an Ivy League school." Labeling and mislabeling don't lead to action. They simply reinforce inertia.

10. *Personalization* confuses "influence with control over others" (Burns, 1980, p. 39). "I never will forgive myself for letting a parent throw a pie in the superintendent's face at our school carnival," said an assistant principal. The superintendent took this unexpected prank in stride and knew that the assistant principal couldn't have controlled the situation anyway.

All of these cognitive distortions are framed in such a way that their holders "pay interest on a debt they don't owe," and in the process waste personal and professional resources that could be better allocated elsewhere. There is also a touch or more of narcissism in the distortions.

The point of this discussion is to raise our consciousness as to the importance of framing what we observe, think, and say in a more rational way, thus minimizing our fear of not controlling the situation and reducing our anxiety in our relationships with ourselves and others. The more we avoid cognitive distortions, the more we are likely to frame our perspectives in a positive way. In the process, we see and release the goodness in others and ourselves, thus being more effective leaders in the role of assistant principal. Why would those we lead want to follow someone who is not positive about possible outcomes?

An assistant principal used the following story to motivate teachers to be positive during a staff-development program. The story makes the point better than any sermon or lecture could, and the surprise ending to the story always brings a smile to the faces of those who hear it.

SNAPSHOT 6.19: THE POWER OF POSITIVE THINKING

Mrs. Birch, the director of food services, sat at a cafeteria table and began to speak about her weekend. "All of you know that I've been a member of a small, rural church. Have been for years. We have a new, young minister fresh out of seminary at Duke University. He is something! He has long hair, he dresses informally, and you won't believe it but he now has a processional and recessional, even though our church choir only has six people in it. He doesn't stand behind the pulpit, but instead walks right out into the congregation to give his sermon.

"And you should see his wife! She dresses like a hippie. She has this long, stringy hair and says pretty much what she thinks and doesn't care who hears it. She could care less about serving at teas in the parsonage, and she has all of these New Age posters she painted displayed on the church walls.

"I'll tell you, they are something! You know why I like them? They are optimistic and that's exactly what this aging congregation needs!"

Your vitality and hopefulness, if not optimism, can be tremendous sources of power as you give leadership to faculty, students, parents, and others. Our research (Brubaker & Coble, 2007a) indicated that problems with interpersonal relationships eroded the assistant principal's credibility, vitality, and optimism (pp. 41–42). Conversely, healthy interpersonal relationships lead to a "can do" school culture and a sense of community where the norm is for persons within the culture to want to teach and lead.

The third way we can react to stress in the assistant principalship is by developing new habits. As one educator put it, take a deep breath and give yourself more life space to breathe and act. This can literally be true, as taking a deep breath gives us time to weigh our feelings and future actions rather than jumping into the fray with a quick response.

Two major questions face you as an assistant principal: How shall I live with myself? How shall we live with each other in the culture of the school? (Brubaker, 2004; Macdonald, 1977). Answering these questions in a way that will help us develop new habits while retaining habits that we already find effective as assistant principals depends on two life forces.

The first of these is the deeply felt conviction that I am always a choice maker. Stated in another way, we are not simply the victims of others' decisions. Let us examine an extreme case that certainly involves a good deal of stress. Imagine for a moment that you are released from your position as an assistant principal. If you are in a victim frame of mind, a natural reaction, you might well elicit sympathy from others by saying that you were the victim of the whims of your bureaucratic superiors, worked in an intolerable situation, and both couldn't and can't do anything about it.

If, on the other hand, you always recognize that you have the power to make decisions, you could well say, "My bureaucratic superiors released me from my position and I've decided to do thus and so in response." In this case, you wouldn't play innocent by pretending that you have no power to respond to the decision to terminate your employment as an assistant principal (1972).

The nonvictim way of thinking and responding is not meant to discount the very real pain and suffering that occur in the world today and to you in this particular situation. Nor is it a rationale for not helping those who are in trouble. It does say that those in dire straits, including yourself, cannot begin to work out of such difficulty until they realize the power of being a choice maker.

A second life source is intentionality. Paul Tillich (1952) argued that "man's vitality is as great as his intentionality" (pp. 81–82). Our intentions as assistant principals naturally flow from our sense of efficacy: "I can make a positive difference" becomes "I will make a difference by doing thus and so."

A third life force evolves from a sense of efficacy and intentionality. It is the power of your personal and organizational vision. Knowing that I can make a difference, and intending to do good things, must be followed by a vision of what is desirable and possible to accomplish. If you don't care where you are going, any trip will do.

What then are some of the specific habits we can develop or reinforce in order to live better with ourselves and others while serving as assistant principals?

We can identify "go-to" activities that will be healthy physically and emotionally for ourselves and others. Simply spending time out of doors is an example. Even spending a few minutes outside can give us new perspective if we are open to all we experience in the process. We are sometimes amazed how stepping outside the school building for a few minutes and deeply breathing in the outside air revives us. An assistant principal shared this understanding with us when giving us a tour of the temporary housing behind the main building.

A regular exercise regimen can serve the same purpose while aiding our respiratory systems and clearing our minds of stress. An assistant principal told us that the half hour she spends on her stationary bike each morning while reading an interesting book gives her a fresh start to each day. Others find walking serves a similar purpose. The list of outdoor hobbies mentioned by our graduate students who are assistant principals seems endless: for example, gardening, sailing, tennis, golf, coaching, cycling, kayaking, canoeing, running, yard work, painting, softball, soccer, and lacrosse.

The arts afford more opportunities to drop out and relax from the stress of work. An assistant principal told us how she and a friend serve as ushers at a nearby university so that they can attend operas, plays, musicals, symphony concerts, and operettas free of charge. They also do this for athletic events.

An assistant principal shared the belief that a trusted friend is invaluable, preferably a person not employed in the same school. She added that she presently has another assistant principal who began in this position the same time that she did. "We have an understanding," she said, "that what we share with each other stays there." Discretion is an essential part of being an effective assistant principal.

Another assistant principal said that her children, although exhausting at times, give her fresh perspective on what is truly important in life. "My little ones," she said, "are discovering the world for the first time and I join them in being amazed by bugs we find, flowers we see while walking together, and trees bent over by the wind. Time with them is totally different from my time at school."

As an assistant principal, you are in a position not only to choose your own stress relievers but also to serve as an example and help create a culture in which teachers and others talk about opportunities they choose to take in order to have more complete and healthy lives. This challenge can be a central theme in professional development activities.

Thomas Newkirk (2009) wrote a seminal article titled "Stress, Control, and the Deprofessionalizing of Teaching" in *Education Week* that was strongly applauded by online respondents. Newkirk wrote:

> When teachers lose control of decision making—when they prepare students for tests they have no role in designing (and often no belief in), when they must abandon units they love because there is no longer time, when they must follow the plans designed by others, when they are locked in systems of instruction and evaluation they don't create or even choose—they will not be relieved of stress.

Their jobs are not made easier, they are made harder and more stressful. As one teacher put it, "The joy is being drained out of teaching." (p. 25)

What is the answer? Newkirk concludes along with other researchers that "those who could make significant decisions probably had a sense of their own agency and control, and this prerogative to act actually made their jobs less stressful than those of workers who largely followed the direction of others" (p. 24). It is important that assistant principals listen, hear, understand, and lead with these powerful thoughts in mind.

As you step into the role of assistant principal during the first days of your administrative career, we wish you the best and hope that this book has been helpful as a guide from the time you imagined yourself as a school administrator to the present-day realities of the assistant principalship. Once again, we invite you to continue our conversation by writing us at the e-mail addresses at the end of the preface.

QUESTIONS FOR DISCUSSION

1. As this chapter is full of examples of how seemingly small things can make a positive difference in the lives of students, teachers, and school administrators, what are some examples of how you have experienced this as a student, teacher, and school leader? What values underlie or are the basis for these examples? For example, "A leader took the time and had the sensitivity to see that I needed some help. This leader often demonstrated respect for the preciousness of other persons."
2. What is your view of the idea that the helper is often helped himself or herself? Illustrate your answer to this question with examples from your own experience.
3. How has your perception of the many and varied activities engaged in by the assistant principal changed, if at all, since you began your principal preparation program? Please give specific examples.
4. Please critique (review, take a position, and support it) the discussion of standardized testing in this chapter. What examples can you give from your own experiences to make your case?
5. What metaphor would you adopt, if any, to describe your school as it is? As it should be? As it can be? See the discussion of metaphors in this chapter to guide your discussion.

6. What guidelines will you follow as an assistant principal in order to work toward a good relationship with the principal? Give examples.

7. What can you do as an assistant principal to implement civilities of leadership as discussed in this chapter in order to improve public relations in your school? Please be specific.

8. What can you do as an assistant principal to help create a culture of leadership in your school that helps all concerned deal with stress in a positive way? Please give concrete examples.

9. How do the cognitive distortions discussed in this chapter speak to your leadership experiences? What can you do to remind yourself of ways to avoid and/or deal better with such distortions?

10. How do the epigraphs at the beginning of this chapter speak to you as you take your first steps in becoming and being a school administrator?

SUGGESTED READINGS

Blasé, J., & Kirby, P. C. (2009). *Bringing out the best in teachers: What effective principals do.* Thousand Oaks, CA: Corwin Press.

Brubaker, D. L. (2004). *Revitalizing curriculum leadership: Inspiring and empowering your school community.* Thousand Oaks, CA: Corwin Press. See chapter 7, "Civility in leadership: The ultimate difference," 105–25.

Brubaker, D. L., & Coble, L. D. (2007a). *Staying on track: An educational leader's guide to preventing derailment and ensuring personal and organizational success.* Thousand Oaks, CA: Corwin Press. See chapter 1, "Accountability and high-stakes testing." See also chapter 7, "The seasons of an educational leader's career."

Darish, J. C. (2004). *Beginning the assistant principalship: A practical guide for new school administrators.* Thousand Oaks, CA: Corwin Press.

Glanz, J. (2004). *The assistant principal's handbook: Strategies for success.* Thousand Oaks, CA: Corwin Press.

Hattie, J. (2008). *Visible learning: A synthesis of over 800 meta-analyses relating to achievement.* New York: Routledge. A seminal work that represent the largest-ever evidence-based research into what actually works in schools to improve learning. A model of teaching and learning based on visible teaching and visible learning is presented. The case is made for the power of directed teaching, feedback, and monitoring within an atmosphere of trust. The author argues that effective teaching takes place when teachers see learning through the eyes of their students.

It follows that effective principals see learning through the eyes of teachers. A must-read book for assistant principals and principals who want to be curriculum and instruction leaders.

Marshall, C., & Hooley, R. M. (2006). *The assistant principal: Leadership choices and challenges.* Thousand Oaks, CA: Corwin Press.

Ramo, J. C. (2009). *The age of the unthinkable: Why the new school disorder constantly surprises us and what we can do about it.* New York: Little, Brown.

Schrum, L., & Levin, B. B. (2009). *Leading 21st-century schools: Harnessing technology for engagement and achievement.* Thousand Oaks, CA: Corwin Press. An excellent, up-to-date resource for school leaders interested in integrating technology into classrooms.

Thomas, R. M. (2005). *High-stakes testing: Coping with collateral damage.* Mahwah, NJ: Lawrence Erlbaum.

Williamson, R. (2009). *Scheduling to improve student learning.* Westerville, OH: National Middle School Association. A topic of interest and concern for all assistant principals and principals. Very well-written.

Williamson, R., & Blackburn, B. R. (2009). *The principalship from A to Z.* Larchmont, NY: Eye on Education. A comprehensive source with an excellent format for each chapter as well as recommended readings and activities.

APPENDIXES

We have developed a number of appendixes that have aided us in leading seminars on the transitional period from teacher to beginning school administrator and beyond. These appendixes may be read and reacted to privately or in a group setting.

Professional development leadership can be an important part of the role you play as a teacher leader, an administrative intern, an assistant principal, and a principal. You will discover that in leading others your own learning in the areas of leadership, curriculum, and instruction will be greatly enhanced. In other words, in the process of helping others, you will also be helped. To recognize this will make you an even better role model for those you lead. Some of these persons are teachers, counselors, and others who may become school administrators.

Please feel free to e-mail us at the addresses at the end of the preface so that we may better understand what happened when you used these materials. We promise a response.

Appendix A: Selecting a School Principal Licensure Program

Please write a number from 1 (low) to 5 (high) to rate how much the following items influence(d) your decision in selecting a principal licensure program. You are encouraged after each item to add further comments that will be useful to you and others in discussion sessions.

_____ 1. Tuition cost. Elaborate:

_____ 2. Geographical location and/or proximity. Elaborate:

_____ 3. Availability of scholarships. Elaborate:

_____ 4. Full-time option. Elaborate:

_____ 5. Part-time option. Elaborate:

_____ 6. Availability of online courses. Elaborate:

_____ 7. Availability of mentors. Elaborate:

_____ 8. Quality field-based experiences, including internships. Elaborate:

___ 9. Attention program gives to curriculum, instruction, and teaching. Elaborate:

___ 10. Balance of academic and managerial aspects of school leadership. Elaborate:

___ 11. Attention given to urban education. Elaborate:

___ 12. Attention given to suburban education. Elaborate:

___ 13. Attention given to rural education. Elaborate:

___ 14. Use of cases and other simulated school projects. Elaborate:

___ 15. Attention given to student achievement in schools. Elaborate:

___ 16. Helpfulness of program's clerical staff in handling your inquiries and paperwork. Elaborate:

___ 17. Program's emphasis on new technologies useful to you as a principal. Elaborate:

___ 18. Opportunity to make the case for being admitted to the program. Elaborate:

Appendix B: The "Table Manners" of Graduate Student Leadership in a Principal Preparation Program

Graduate school can be among the more enjoyable and rewarding experiences you can have. You are introduced to new ideas and practices. An opportunity to reflect on and integrate learning in relation to previous experiences is afforded. You encounter many persons with varying backgrounds, talents, interests, and aspirations—the substance of personal growth.

One value of graduate school education is the opportunity to demonstrate maturity and self-direction. Professors, instructors, and school administrators are vehicles to assist in this growth and development. The following guidelines are designed to facilitate clear student-instructor communication and enhance leadership skills and attitudes. Please use a magic marker to highlight the guidelines and ideas that speak to you. Then, if possible, please use these guidelines to stimulate discussion.

Basic assumptions faculty often bring to this process:

Graduate students should play a proactive role, not simply a reactive one.

As part of program planning, students should be familiar with the preparatory program's guidelines, rules, and regulations.

Graduate students should demonstrate maturity by recognizing the importance of due dates and meeting them.

If a substantive reaction to student writing is called for on the part of an instructor, graduate students should negotiate this well in advance.

When a student submits a written document to an instructor, clean copy is required. Use a good copy editor or proofreader to ensure this.

Open communication, rather than "hidden agendas," is the key to mutual respect and consideration.

The scholarly responsibility a student assumes in preparation for and in reaction to class is an important responsibility.

Effective oral and written communication is key to successful graduate student leadership in the preparation program and beyond.

Removing and minimizing "irritants" leads to a better relationship with instructors.

As part of the negotiation process, graduate students and instructors should clearly state their expectations.

If you want satisfaction as a graduate student:

Be sure to ask for the instructor's e-mail address if this is not in the course syllabus.

With regard to telephone calls to the instructor, if the professor isn't in, leave your name, telephone number, the nature of your business, and the best time to return your call.

For efficient and effective use of your time, prepare for the content of the telephone conversation.

Identify yourself at the onset of the conversation on the phone.

When substantive agreements are arrived at over the telephone, the graduate student should follow up with an e-mail or memorandum of understanding, concluding with "Unless I hear from you otherwise, I'll assume this is correct."

Don't have a secretary, in the event that you have one, place calls to instructors that put faculty members on hold until the caller is available to talk.

Remember to copy appropriate parties via e-mail or memoranda.

In some cases, give a self-addressed, stamped envelope to the instructor for a sure response.

Log important contacts with instructors with date, time, and outline of content in your log.

Clearly state what you expect of the instructor when corresponding with him or her.

It is probably wise to use a fairly formal style when e-mailing an instructor.

Appendix C:
The Power of Critique

Critique is the lifeblood of reflection and decision making for the school administrator and the graduate student in a principal preparation program. Critique is sometimes defined as the art or practice of criticism. Critique can be much more than this deficit definition, which focuses on what is wrong or missing. Critique occurs when a person (a) reviews what has taken place, (b) adopts a point of view (thesis) as to what took place, and (c) supports this point of view or thesis. Please give examples of your engagement in critique during a typical workday:

_____

_____

_____

What are some of the subtle dynamics involved in bringing excellence to critique? The first is discernment. To discern is to see clearly or differentiate the important from the less important. Making such a judgment always depends on a particular context, the situation in which the decision is made. In other words, one must move beyond generalizations to describe clearly the particulars of what is happening within a context.

A field experience observed by a student in a principal preparation program serves as an example. Paul is a seventh grader who is called to the assistant principal's office for possessing metallic knuckles. The assistant principal knows that metallic knuckles are considered a weapon—an offense that carries a ten-day, out-of-school suspension.

The assistant principal is aware that this is a first offense for Paul, as well as the fact that Paul is living with his grandmother because his father is in jail and Paul's alcoholic mother is living with a drug addict. In fact, Paul got the metallic knuckles from this man. The assistant principal, the school resource officer, Paul, and Paul's grandmother had a lengthy discussion during which Paul was visibly shaken by the gravity of what he had done.

The assistant principal's demeanor demonstrated his serious attitude toward the situation. At the same time, the assistant principal was sensitive to the context of Paul's home life and the role that the school context could play in relating to Paul. The assistant principal, on consultation with the principal and the school resource officer, decided to give Paul a three-day, in-school suspension with the understanding that a second offense would automatically kick in a ten-day, out-of-school suspension.

Please briefly describe one or more situations in which you used discernment within a particular context to reach what you considered a fair and reasonable decision.

Appendix D: Dealing with Contradictions in Principal Preparation Programs and Beyond

Arthur M. Schlesinger Jr. (2000) notes that conflict, freedom, change, and discovery are essential ingredients in a democracy: "So long as society stays free, so long will it continue in a state of tension, breeding *contradiction*, breeding strife. But, conflict is also the guarantee of freedom; it is the instrument of change; it is above all, the source of discovery, the source of art, the source of love" (pp. 521–22; italics ours).

"Contradiction" comes from the Latin *contra* (against) + *dicere* or *dictus* (to say). For our purposes, contradiction is the act of saying or doing the opposite of something already said or done.

Two kinds of contradictions facing the graduate student in a principal preparation program and the beginning educational administrator are the basis for the following exercise. These contradictions are (1) those one chooses to celebrate and (2) those one chooses to try to reconcile. (We talk about problem *solving* and dilemma *reconciling*.)

Please identify those contradictions that you face or might face as a graduate student in a principal preparatory program that are to be celebrated and those that you choose to try to reconcile.

Column 1 (celebrate)   Column 2 (reconcile)

Completed Examples

Column 1 (celebrate)
One of my instructors is younger than
I am but the instructor's
instruction and rich experiences are
admirable and helpful.

Column 2 (reconcile)
I feel like I have one foot in my
teaching during the day
and the other in my principal
preparation program at night.

I celebrate my abilities as a graduate
student but I have learned to keep
this to myself.

My instructors respect confidence
but my fellow graduate students
sometimes read this as arrogance.

Please identify those experiences you face or might face as a beginning educational administrator that are to be celebrated and those experiences you face or might face that you will try to reconcile.

Column 1 (celebrate)

Column 2 (reconcile)

Completed Examples

Column 1 (celebrate)
We have excellent parent involvement
and this means we give many of our
resources (time and effort) to parents.

Column 2 (reconcile)
As an assistant principal I always
feel like the person in the middle.

I appreciate the energy of young
colleagues even though it makes me
feel old at times.

There are always more desires
(wants) than resources, but many
times when they are expressed I
realize our limitations.

Appendix E: The Joy of Teaching and Leading

Please list three things about teaching that you especially liked.

_____

_____

_____

Please list three things about your beginning leadership as a school administrator that you think you will especially like.

_____

_____

_____

Compare and contrast these two lists. Discuss similarities and differences in the two lists.

Appendix F: Working Alone and Working in a Team

A principal preparation program and a school are alike in that they recognize democratic tenets of valuing autonomy (working alone) and working as a part of a team. It is a challenge in both settings to find the most satisfying balance between these two ways of operating. The following items may be applied to two settings: your principal preparation program and your beginning as a school administrator.

There are times when I enjoy working alone. Some of these times are . . .

Some of the reasons why I enjoy working alone are . . .

There are times when I don't enjoy working alone. Instead, I want to be with others as part of a team. Some of these times are . . .

Some of the reasons why I enjoy working on a team are . . .

How do you know when you are a team member? Please place a check in front of the items you support.

___ I recognize that what I do affects others on the team as well as those that the team influences.

___ No one on the team projects the feeling that he or she is better than others.

___ I am privately and publicly willing to acknowledge other team members' talents and contributions.

___ I rarely feel lonely.

___ I rarely feel down but instead feel lifted up by other team members.

___ I feel energized.

___ I discover human and nonhuman resources I didn't know I had.

___ I have the courage to do what I think is right.

___ My vision for the future is sharpened, thus motivating myself and others.

___ I can agree and disagree with team members without taking this personally.

___ I can try out or practice new ideas and skills while having a safety net of team members to support me.

___ I am encouraged to take risks that I otherwise would be reluctant to take.

___ People with more status than I have encouraged and rewarded me for being a team member.

___ Members of the team celebrate my victories.

___ Members of the team may well become my friends as well as my professional colleagues.

Appendix G: A Personal Leadership Change and Conservation Inventory

What are three things about *my leadership* that I highly value and want to conserve?

_____

_____

_____

What are three things—challenges—about *my leadership* that I want to change?

_____

_____

_____

Appendix H: Traits of Outstanding Leaders

After a situation in which principal preparation students heard a guest speaker talk about outstanding leaders, they were asked to tell a story about an experience they had when an administrator was brilliant or superior as a leader. We then listed the qualities they identified. Please use the following checklist to characterize a leader who you thought was brilliant or superior in a situation you've experienced.

_____   _____
Leader's Name   Leadership Position

___ used applied intelligence (high-level common sense)
___ was authoritative (had a sense of presence and knew his/her stuff)
___ did his or her homework (facts and frameworks/context well in hand)
___ was an expert planner (left situation with concrete next steps in mind)
___ had a sense of purpose (vision) stated clearly and referred to when appropriate
___ was clearly committed to what needed to be done
___ listened well and spoke to persons at their levels of expertise
___ was fair
___ was authentic or genuine (not phony)
___ was compassionate (not patronizing) and sensitive

___ was not mean-spirited; has a sense of humor
___ was willing to take risks (to make himself or herself vulnerable)
___ conveyed a sense of trust or attitude that others can do what needs to be done
___ was able to bracket self (stand back) and look at situation with objectivity
___ held the good of the organization as a primary consideration
___ was able to build partnerships

Appendix I: Job Interviewing and the Creation of Learning Communities

You are being interviewed. The interviewer says, "Interviewers usually ask, 'What have you done or accomplished in your previous leadership position?' My question is somewhat different: What did you learn in your previous position and how did this contribute to the creation of learning communities?" How will you respond?

Appendix J: Conveying a Belief in Self in a Job Interview and Beyond

One of the main things that interviewers look for and sense in a promising candidate is belief in self. Pat Conroy (2002), a well-known author, looks back on his experience as a basketball player at The Citadel in amazement and shares with us his view that "belief in oneself—authentic, inviolable, and unshakable belief, not the undercutting kind—is necessary to all human achievement. Once I began believing in myself and not listening to the people who did not believe in me, I turned myself into a point guard who you needed to watch" (p. 398).

Please list the people and their actions that helped you achieve this authentic belief in self.

_____

_____

_____

_____

Please list the people and their actions that worked against your achieving authentic belief in self.

_____

_____

_____

_____

Finally, please list any advice you can give to others in order to help them achieve authentic belief in self. In other words, what lessons learned can you share with them on this matter?

_____

_____

_____

_____

_____

Appendix K: What Works and Doesn't Work in Doing Professional Development

The appendixes or exercises in this section of the book have been written in part for professional development leaders. You may do this exercise alone or in a small group. If you are in a small group setting, name (a) a facilitator and (b) a note taker or reporter.

Please *identify* and *place in priority order* three things you've discovered do work well in doing professional development and three things that don't work well in doing professional development. (Priority order refers to the strength of response.)

Three things that work well in doing professional development:

_____

_____

_____

Three things that don't work well in doing professional development:

_____

_____

_____

Appendix L: Preparing to Give Leadership to Educational Reform Efforts

You have probably been primarily in the reactor role with regard to educational reform efforts. The federal government, state departments of public instruction, and other institutions have expected you to fall in line as they issue mandates and expect them to be implemented. Other reform efforts have been initiated by school boards and newly appointed superintendents of schools eager to gain approval as soon as possible, often in order to move up the ladder to more prestigious positions in new communities.

As you gain more positional authority in administrative positions, you will be forced into a more active and responsible role with regard to educational reform. In fact, you will be introducing reform efforts in your school, some of which will seem fairly inconsequential to you but not to your teachers and staff. It is these efforts introduced by you that are addressed in this exercise. We have found this exercise to be very useful in stimulating discussion in our professional development activities.

The following minimal criteria for proceeding with a reform effort were constructed by Seymour B. Sarason, professor emeritus at Yale University and author of *Educational Reform: A Self-Scrutinizing Memoir* (2002). He poses a number of questions central to your leadership as you participate in educational reform efforts.

Sarason introduces his key questions with an overall question: "What are the minimal criteria by which you will decide whether to proceed with a reform effort, or so to speak, forget it?" He adds, "Enthusiasm, a high level of motivation, a laudable desire to rectify or improve an unsatisfactory state of affairs, a vision of what can and should be—these, like love, are not enough, hence the astronomical divorce rate and dispiriting reform failures" (p. 113). Sarason's key questions follow (pp. 113–14).

"What is distinctively different about the setting in which you seek to effect a change?" For example, what are the formal and informal power arrangements with others in your school, such as fellow administrators, teacher leaders, and staff members? It may seem like a minor matter to you to implement a more efficient organizational change in the cafeteria, but it is considered a major matter by cafeteria workers and some teachers. It may seem of little consequence to you to have teaching assistants sit with children in the cafeteria in the place of teachers, but it is not of little consequence to teaching assistants.

"Do you have criteria and ways to determine the degree to which those who are the objects of change see a need for change?" Ideally, those who are involved in the change invite you to make it, but this is frequently not the case, thus making it a challenge for you to clearly communicate your criteria for moving ahead with the change. Knowing the key persons with high credibility in your school, persons who must initially be won over, is an important first step. If they own the decision about the need for a change and the plan for its acceptance and implementation, the skids have been greased. If not, trouble is surely ahead.

"Have you built into the change process meetings or forums in which you and the participants review and assess what has happened or has been accomplished or not?" Formative evaluation of progress made and not made continues the feeling of ownership by key leaders and others involved in the change process. Much formative evaluation is backstage and informal, often on a one-to-one basis.

"Because you know, you certainly should know, that one source of failure of a reform effort is that a person in a key role—such as the principal or superintendent—has decided to leave, what agreement should you seek that gives you a role in selecting a replacement?" Followers often feel "jerked around" by a sudden changing of the guard, the result being that the next fad or "flavor of the month" is just around the corner. Calling on any sources of power you have, such as charisma, succor, and expertise, is the key to whatever continuity is possible when leadership changes are made. (See appendix O, "Sources of Power Available to You as an Educational Leader and Decision Maker.")

"Given the above questions, and assuming that you have dealt with them conceptually and realistically, do you have the funding, personnel, and time to do justice to the implications of these questions?" New and difficult financial realities sometimes eliminate support for a program in the blink of an eye. At other times, funds and therefore personnel appear when unexpected— particularly at the end of a budget year. The key is to seize opportunities, not simply take them.

Appendix M: How Good (and Comfortable) Are You as a Public Speaker and Listener?

Public speaking is an important part of your presentation of self as an educational leader. The following self-inventory is a good starting place as you work to improve your public-speaking and listening skills. You may also wish to have a trusted colleague and perhaps others assess your skills.

It is interesting to note that you are more comfortable with some skills than others, and you are more proficient with some skills than others. With practice, we become more comfortable and proficient.

Please assess your comfort and proficiency from 1 (low) to 5 (high) on the following items.

Comfort   Proficiency

Speaking one-on-one
Listening one-on-one
Answering questions one-on-one
Speaking to a small group
Listening (as the speaker/leader) to verbal and
    nonverbal language of the small group
Answering questions after speaking to a small group
Speaking to a large group
Listening (as the speaker/leader) to verbal and
    nonverbal language of the large group

	Comfort	*Proficiency*
Answering questions after speaking to a large group		
Telephone interviews		
Television interviews		
Radio interviews		
Newspaper interviews		

Appendix N: Guidelines for Going on Television

The media have given attention to schools and schooling in two major ways: crises and the quick fix (get fad X in all schools in order to fix the problem). Administrators increasingly need to understand the role of media in modern society and how they must be prepared, often at a moment's notice, to react to it. Television, with its 24/7 news coverage, is especially challenging for educational leaders. In order to prepare yourself for going on television, please use the following checklist. Graduate students have found the checklist useful in assessing how educational leaders they view on television perform.

_____ 1. Talk to the reporter, not the camera or microphone. (Look the reporter straight in the eye.)

_____ 2. Stand or sit erectly. Don't stoop or bend over.

_____ 3. If you say, "No comment," add that you will get back to the reporter by such and such a time.

_____ 4. Know who you're dealing with and develop rapport with the reporter when possible.

_____ 5. Remember that the good photographer (cameraperson) doesn't have the camera to his or her eye. The camera can be rolling from any position, even if it is under his or her arm.

_____ 6. Be politely on guard all of the time.

_____ 7. Take advantage of the nonconfrontational good news programs.

____ 8. The bottom line is to meet reporters head-on and be honest. The camera doesn't lie. It will see the eyes.

____ 9. Be cool and confident. It disarms reporters.

____ 10. Remember that there is a high degree of sensitivity about minorities and women at this time in the history of our nation.

____ 11. A smile is the most disarming thing in the world. Bring to the camera the real person inside you.

____ 12. Be prepared. If you don't know, say, "I don't know."

____ 13. There is no such thing as "off the record." Beware of the reporter who says, "This is off the record."

____ 14. You can ask to talk to the reporter about something before you go on camera. If the reporter won't allow you to do this, don't talk.

____ 15. It is a good idea to suggest a place for the interview. Get an appropriate visual backdrop.

____ 16. Watch hazards around you. Don't swivel in a chair. Don't fidget. Calm down, even if it means that you grab a desk in front of you or behind you.

____ 17. Take your time.

____ 18. Ask to reshoot if you are extremely dissatisfied with the interview.

____ 19. Limit the number of remarks and focus on two or three major points.

____ 20. Ask the reporter both whom he or she has talked to and whom he or she will talk to before the story is over.

____ 21. You can occasionally stop a reporter dead in his or her tracks by saying, "I have no earthly idea what you're talking about."

____ 22. The school or central office is private property. Be aware, however, that television cameras can shoot onto your property from a nearby site without your permission.

Appendix O: Sources of Power Available to You as an Educational Leader and Decision Maker

Malcolm Gladwell, author of the best-selling *The Tipping Point*, *Blink*, and *Outliers: The Story of Success*, shared the following with us in an interview by Jennifer Reingold (2008): "Successful people are people who have made the most of a series of gifts that have been given to them by their culture or their history. Instead of thinking about it as something that you acquire, talent should be thought of as something that you develop" (p. 160, 162).

This is consistent with our view of creative leadership. We define creative leadership as using your talents to help others identify and use their talents (Brubaker, 2004, pp. 89–91). In using our talents to help others identify and use their talents, there are several sources of power we can draw upon. Please discuss ways in which you draw upon these sources of power as a graduate student seeking principal certification and as a beginning administrator in a school.

Positional authority is power by virtue of one's position in the organization. It is commonly associated with bureaucratic forms of organization, for those with more positional authority give commands to their subordinates, who have less. Regardless of the respect, or lack of it, accorded the person with positional authority, the bureaucratic subordinate is expected to obey such commands.

Traditionally, it has been drawn upon heavily, but observers in the area of leadership education argue that drawing on positional authority is much like

143

using a battery: the more you use it, the less there is to use in the future. They therefore recommend that positional authority should be suspended by the leader whenever possible and used judiciously when appropriate.

Expertise is a source of power attributed to persons because of their recognized ability to do something well. An assistant principal, for example, may be recognized as a well-organized person who has demonstrated expertise in writing reports. She is therefore asked to head the accreditation planning team for the school. The ability to organize and articulate ideas is an important kind of expertise essential to the leadership process. Developing one's expertise is hard work, something frequently overlooked by those who say, "It's easy for her." In fact, the person who is really good at something simply makes it *look* easy.

Succor is an informal kind of power that leaves others with the feeling that they are supported emotionally. It is commonly associated with counseling and coaching. "You can do it" is the message transmitted. Leaders sometimes reach the place in the planning process where they are ready to give up because of a lack of interest on the part of committee members or opposition from a person or group. It is precisely at this point that succor can give momentum to tasks that must be completed. The morale of the group depends on this kind of support.

Charisma is a sort of magnetic charm often equated with sex appeal. Nonverbal messages, such as smiles and nods of approval, are the vehicles of communication used by the charismatic leader. Style of dress and the leader's bearing give added charisma at times.

George F. Will (2009) advises us that decision making often depends on patience: "Charisma is less potent than the smitten imagine; endurance is not sufficient, but is necessary" (p. A13). He adds that in most organizations "80 percent of the important work is done by a talented 20 percent. And 95 percent of the work is done . . . out of sight, where strong convictions leavened by good humor are the currency of accomplishment" (p. A13). Will uses Ted Kennedy as an example of such patience and endurance. There is, in other words, significant research that indicates that charismatic leaders rarely "boost performance in the long term" (Reingold, 2008, p. 146).

Appendix P: Some Thoughts on Professional Development Leadership

1. It is important to create the best plans and professional development learning materials possible, but they should be viewed as a springboard for learning rather than ends in themselves. The inclination is often to try to create perfect plans and materials, but what happens when they are implemented or used should be used to reconstruct them.

2. It is the ongoing evaluation and revision of plans and materials that stimulates the professional development leader to learn more. It is this reconstruction of knowledge that serves as a model for persons influenced by the leader. (In this sense the leader has to "get" to "give" to others.)

3. In our society, the personality of the individual is often emphasized at the expense of the personality of the setting, group, and organization. The professional development leader is wise to recognize this reality and its implications for professional development leadership. For example, the assistant principal's relationship with a team leader on the faculty may be quite different from the assistant principal's relationship with an advisory council of team leaders.

4. When a problem arises in a setting, it is easy to try to fix it with simple cause-effect thinking. For example, George is a problem in a faculty meeting. Get rid of George and you get rid of the problem. In fact, the setting is a transactional context in which all within the setting relate to each other in order to meet their needs and desires based on personal histories.

Removing George from the setting does not keep the same or other problems from emerging.

5. Formal leadership in a setting is rather easily identified. Informal leadership is more subtle and nuanced. The wise professional development leader recognizes this reality and finds ways to identify, develop, and coordinate the talents of others in a variety of settings. For example, the assistant principal may engage in a conversation with a teacher during lunch that leads to the teacher working with a colleague in order to help him or her become more positive during faculty meetings.

6. The perceptive professional development leader tempers first impressions with emerging realities. For example, the assistant principal may discover that a teacher who appeared to be shy is an outspoken leader during an advisory council meeting.

7. There can be an important difference between someone who is an *official* in an organization and someone who is *officious*. The latter is meddlesome; the former can offer opportunities. For example, the assistant principal who always tells people that he or she is the assistant principal is being officious. Being the assistant principal with official responsibilities affords you the ability to use your discretionary power. The assistant principal as professional development leader is usually at his or her best when he or she blends in with those being led—that is, when he or she serves as more of a colleague than a bureaucratic superior.

Appendix Q: Sample Candidate Resume

Janet Jones
222 Elm Street
Central City USA
777.222.2222
jjones@exampleofresume.com

OBJECTIVE

To utilize my strengths, as well as the strengths of others, to foster the continued growth and development of all stakeholders as assistant principal of Central City High School.

SUMMARY

- Instructional leader who has benefited from completing a full-time principal internship fulfilling the role of an assistant principal
- Dynamic, self-motivated professional with a genuine interest in students' academic and social growth and experience in elementary, middle, and high school education
- Key strengths include community and partnership development, classroom management, assessment analysis, program development, and instructional leadership

PROFESSIONAL EXPERIENCE

Central City Middle School, Central City USA

Administrative Intern—November 20XX–Present

- Visited classrooms daily and provided feedback to teachers
- Conferenced with students concerning behavior referrals
- Coordinated the USA Competency Test and formative tests
- Met weekly with administrative team to plan short- and long-range goals
- Performed various managerial/supervision duties including cafeteria, athletic events, and common areas
- Managed exceptional children's database
- Member of Leadership Team

Central City Elementary School

Administrative Intern—August 20XX–October 20XX

- Developed new teacher induction program
- Dialogued with teachers after classroom visits and offered specific instructional feedback
- Modeled lessons for beginning teachers
- Helped teachers develop growth plans
- Served as administrative liaison to reading department
- Performed various managerial/supervision duties including buses, cafeteria, and athletic events
- Member of Leadership Team and Curriculum and Instruction Team

University of Central City USA

Curriculum and Instruction Internship Supervisor—August 20XX–May 20XX

- Supervised, through classroom observations, undergraduates enrolled in beginning teacher class at UCC and conferenced with students regarding their placements
- Coordinated, with principals, the placement of student interns at Central City Middle School and Central City Elementary School
- Planned and led weekly development for middle school interns

Central City Elementary School, Central City, USA

Fifth-Grade Teacher—19XX–20XX

- Designed differentiated approaches to enhance student learning
- Designed lessons aligned with USA curriculum and pacing guides
- Worked closely with exceptional children's teacher using an inclusion model
- Managed classroom through effective discipline
- Developed positive relationships with students and parents to foster learning

Other Duties

- Mentor, 20XX–20XX
- School Improvement Leadership Team member, 20XX–20XX
- Curriculum Committee member, 19XX–20XX; cochair, 20XX–20XX
- Peer observer, 20XX–20XX
- Student Intervention Team cochair, 19XX–20XX
- Climate Committee cochair, 20XX–20XX
- Scheduling Committee cochair, 20XX–20XX

PROFESSIONAL DEVELOPMENT

- Presenter, Central City University Orientation Program, October 20XX
- Participant, national conference, Association of Supervision and Curriculum Development, Eastend, USA, March 20XX
- Participant, Data for Instructional Improvement, Westend, USA, March 20XX

PROFESSIONAL RECOGNITION

- 20XX Central City Civic Club Young Educator of the Year
- 20XX–20XX Central City Elementary Teacher of the Year

EDUCATION

University of Central City, Central City, USA
Master of School Administration, May 20XX

Highlands University, Highland Heights, USA
Bachelor of Arts, May 19XX
Major: English
Licensures: K–6 Teaching and Reading

PROFESSIONAL AFFILIATIONS

- Member, USA Association of School Administrators
- Member, USA Principal and Assistant Principal Association

References

Amme, R. D. (2003). The lost art of listening. *Media Crisis Management*, 1–5. Retrieved from www.amme.com

Amme, R. D. (2007, September 14). Watch out when you get communications training. *Amme & Associates Newsletter*, 1.

Angelou, M. (2009, December 7). The take. *Newsweek*, 27.

Blasé, J., & Kirby, P. C. (2009). *Bringing out the best in teachers: What effective principals do.* Thousand Oaks, CA: Corwin Press.

Bolman, L. G., & Deal, T. E. (2002). *Reframing the path to school leadership: A guide for teachers and principals.* Thousand Oaks, CA: Corwin Press.

Brubaker, D. L. (2004). *Revitalizing curriculum leadership: Inspiring and empowering your school community* (2nd ed.). Thousand Oaks, CA: Corwin Press. First edition (1994) titled *Creative curriculum leadership: Inspiring and empowering your school community.*

Brubaker, D. L. (2006). *The charismatic leader: The presentation of self and the creation of educational settings.* Thousand Oaks, CA: Corwin Press.

Brubaker, D. L., & Coble, L. D. (2005). *The hidden leader: Leadership lessons on the potential within.* Thousand Oaks, CA: Corwin Press.

Brubaker, D. L., & Coble, L. D. (2007a). *Staying on track: An educational leader's guide to preventing derailment and ensuring personal and organizational success* (2nd ed.). Thousand Oaks, CA: Corwin Press. First edition 1997.

Brubaker, D. L., & Coble, L. D. (2007b). *Teacher renewal: Stories of inspiration to balance your life.* Clemmons, NC: On Track Press.

Burns, D. D. (1980). *Feeling good.* New York: Signet.

Chittister, J. (2008). *The gift of years: Growing older gracefully.* New York: BlueBridge.

Coble, L. D., Clodfelter, M. H., & Brubaker, D. L. (2007). *Strategies for your improvement: A developmental guide for educational leader utilizing 360° feedback.* Greensboro, NC: MCO Leadership Associates.

Conroy, P. (2002). *My losing season.* Garden City, NJ: Doubleday.

Darish, J. C. (2004). *Beginning the assistant principalship: A practical guide for new school administrators.* Thousand Oaks, CA: Corwin Press.

Darling-Hammond, L. (2007, January 10). A Marshall Plan for teaching: What it will take to leave No Child Left Behind. *Education Week, 28,* 48.

Fitzgerald, F. S. (1936, March). The crack-up. *Esquire,* 72. Reprinted 1993. New York: New Directions Publishing Corporation.

Foote, D. (2008, October 11). Lessons from Locke. *Newsweek,* 47.

Fullan, M. (2008, April 9). School leadership's unfinished agenda: Integrating individual and organizational development. *Education Week, 36,* 28.

Gallagher, J. J. (2007, April 4). Reform's missing ingredient: Building a high-quality support system for education. *Education Week, 27,* 29.

Gardner, H. (1993). *Multiple intelligences: The theory in practice.* New York: Basic.

Gardner, H. (2000). *Intelligence reframed: Multiple intelligences for the twenty-first century.* New York: Basic.

Gewertz, C. (2007, March 28). Poll finds gaps in outlooks of teachers, principals. *Education Week,* 5.

Gibran, K. (1923). *The prophet.* New York: Knopf.

Gladwell, M. (2008). *Outliers: The story of success.* New York: Little, Brown & Co.

Glanz, J. (2004). *The assistant principal's handbook: Strategies for success.* Thousand Oaks, CA: Corwin Press.

Goffman, E. (1959). *The presentation of self in everyday life.* New York: Doubleday Anchor.

Goffman, E. (1967). *Interaction ritual: Essays on face-to-face behavior.* New York: Doubleday Anchor.

Goffman, E. (1974). *Frame analysis: An essay on the organization of experience.* Cambridge, MA: Harvard University.

Hattie, John (2008). *Visible learning: A synthesis of over 800 meta-analyses relating to achievement.* New York: Routledge.

Hess, F. M., & Kelly, A. P. (2005). The accidental principal. *Education Next, 5*(3), 34–40.

Hess, F. M., & Kelly, A. P. (2007). Learning to lead: What gets taught in principal preparation programs. *Teachers College Record, 109*(1), 244–74.

Honawar, V. (2007, March 28). Curriculum-development group urges focus shift to whole child. *Education Week,* 7.

Jacoby, S. (2008). *The age of American unreason.* New York: Pantheon Books.

Klein, J. (2002). *The natural.* New York: Doubleday.

Kleinfield, S. (1989). *The hotel.* New York: Simon & Schuster.

Lowry, T. (2008, July 7). Charter schools get the test scores up. *Business Week.* Retrieved from www.businessweek.com/bwdaily/dnflash/content/jul2008077_836070.htm, 1–2.

Macdonald, J. B. (1977, December). Interview conducted by Ruth Fairfield at the University of North Carolina at Greensboro.

Marshall, C., & Hooley, R. M. (2006). *The assistant principal: Leadership choices and challenges* (2nd ed.). Thousand Oaks, CA: Corwin Press.

Matthews, C. (2008, January 18). Hard Ball. *MSNBC.*

May, R. (1972). *Power and innocence.* New York: Norton.

McCall, M., Lombardo, M., & Morrison, A. (1988). *The lessons of experience.* Lexington, MA: Lexington Books.

McCourt, F. (2005). *Teacher man.* New York: Scribner.

National Association of Secondary School Principals (NASSP). (2005). *Developing the 21st century school principal.* Reston, VA: NASSP.

Newkirk, T. (2009, October 21). Stress, Control, and the Deprofessionalizing of Teaching. *Education Week,* 24–25.

Noddings, N. (2007, March 21). The new anti-intellectualism in America. *Education Week*, 29, 32.

Olson, L. (2007, September 12). Getting serious about preparation. *Education Week*, S3–S12.

Peck, M. S. (1978). *The road less traveled.* New York: Simon & Schuster.

Peck, M. S. (1993). *A world waiting to be born: Civility rediscovered.* New York: Bantam.

Pitts, L., Jr. (2007, November 1). All the news FEMA wants you to have. *Greensboro News & Record*, A9.

Quindlen, A. (2005, October 24). The value of the outsider. *Newsweek*, 86.

Rae-Dupree, J. (2008, May 4). Can you become a creature of new habits? *New York Times*, 4.

Ramo, J. C. (2009). *The age of the unthinkable: Why the new world disorder constantly surprises us and what we can do about it.* New York: Little, Brown & Co.

Reingold, J. (2008, November 24). Meet your new leader. *Fortune*, 145–46.

Reingold, J. (2008, November 24). Secrets of their success. *Fortune*, 160, 162.

Resnick, A. M. (2007, March 7). Educatocracy. *Education Week*, 24–25.

Sarason, S. B. (1972). *The creation of educational settings and the future societies.* San Francisco: Jossey-Bass.

Sarason, S. B. (2002). *Educational reform: A self-scrutinizing memoir.* San Francisco: Jossey-Bass.

Sarason, S. B. (2009, September 3). Telephone conversation with Dale L. Brubaker.

Schlesinger, A., Jr. (2000). *Journals: 1952–2000.* New York: Penguin Press.

Schrum, L., & Levin, B. B. (2009). *Leading 21st-century schools: Harnessing technology for engagement and achievement.* Thousand Oaks, CA: Corwin Press.

Senge, P. (1990). *The fifth discipline: The art and practice of the learning organization.* New York: Doubleday.

Shulman, L. S. (1993, November/December). Teaching as community property: Putting an end to pedagogical solitude. *Change*, 6–7.

Smith, H. (1988). *The power game.* New York: Random House.

Steinem, G. (1992). *Revolution from within: A book of self-esteem.* Boston: Little, Brown.

Tell, C. (2001, February). Appreciating good teaching. *Educational Leadership, 58,* 6–11.

Thomas, R. M. (2005). *High-stakes testing: Coping with collateral damage.* Mahwah, NJ: Lawrence Erlbaum.

Tillich, P. (1952). *The courage to be.* New Haven, CT: Yale University Press.

University of North Carolina at Greensboro (2009). *Graduate school catalogue,* www.uncg.edu/elc/msa.html, 1–2.

Welch, J., & Welch, S. (2008, December 8). Release your inner extrovert. *Business Week,* 92.

Will, G. F. (2008, April 27). 25 years later, nation remains at risk. *Greensboro News & Record,* H6.

Will, G. F. (2009, August 27). Ted Kennedy: A positive balance. *Greensboro News & Record,* A13.

Williams, M. (2009). Investigating sustained staff development on the performance of assistant principals in their current roles and as newly appointed principals. Research proposal, University of North Carolina at Greensboro.

Williamson, R. (2009). *Scheduling to improve student learning.* Westerville, OH: National Middle School Association.

Williamson, R., & Blackburn, B. R. (2009). *The principalship from A to Z.* Larchmont, NY: Eye on Education.

Index

136–38, 145–46; dealing with stress, 98–111; by example, 74–76; ISLLC's *Educational Leadership Policy Standards*, 34–35; Personal Leadership Change and Conservation Inventory, 129; recent shift in school leadership role, 33; Traits of Outstanding Leaders, 130–31; University of North Carolina's Department of Educational Leadership and Cultural Foundations, 36–38

leading by example, 74–76

Leithwood, Kenneth, 63

licensure exam, 15

licensure program, 37; selection of, 117–18

local (district) requirements, for principal certification, 33, 38

Lombardo, M., 26

loneliness, 8; new student in middle school, example of, 64–65; solitude at the top, 81–82. *See also* team membership

luxury hotel metaphor, 90, 93–94

Macdonald, James B., 77

magnification, minimization and, 106

Marshall, Catherine, 23, 26, 58–59, 63, 68

master's in school administration (MSA) program: applicants for, 2, 5, 7, 27–29; certification tied to, 34; changes in course content, 37–38; length of time allowed for, 36; self-pacing during, 32–33; as springboard for composing inner curriculum, 33–39; University of North Carolina's, 36–38. *See also* principal preparation programs

Matthews, Chris, 13

McCall, M., 26

McCourt, Frank, 23, 24

memorandum: on job description for internship, 44, 50; log important contacts with instructors, 121; of understanding between graduate student and instructor, 120

men: grooming, 59; school as patriarchy, 73; women deferring to, 9

mental filter, 105

mentor availability: as criteria for choosing licensure program, 117–18; during internship, 45

metaphors, for school/schooling, 73–76, 90, 93–94; conflicting, 77–82

Miller's Analogy Test, 36

"mind-reading," 105–6

minimization, magnification and, 106

mislabeling, 106

Morrison, A., 26

mourning phase, 17

Moynihan, Patrick, 51

MSA. *See* master's in school administration

multiple intelligences, 26

Murphy, Joseph, 34

mutual assessment, 57–60

MySpace, 49

National Board Certification for Principals, 35

National Board for Professional Teaching Standards (NBPTS), 36

National School Boards Association, 82

national standards, for principal certification, 34–35

NBPTS. *See* National Board for Professional Teaching Standards

About the Authors

Dale L. Brubaker is professor emeritus of educational leadership and cultural studies at the University of North Carolina at Greensboro. He has also served on the faculties of the University of California–Santa Barbara and the University of Wisconsin–Milwaukee. He received his doctorate from Michigan State University. He is the author or coauthor of numerous books on education and educational leadership, including *Curriculum Planning: The Dynamics of Theory and Practice; Theses and Dissertations: A Guide to Planning, Research, and Writing; Avoiding Thesis and Dissertation Pitfalls; Staying on Track: An Educational Leader's Guide to Preventing Derailment and Ensuring Personal Success; Revitalizing Curriculum Leadership: Inspiring and Empowering Your School Community; The Charismatic Leader: The Presentation of Self and the Creation of Educational Settings;* and *The Hidden Leader: Leadership Lessons on the Potential Within.*

Misti Williams is clinical assistant professor of educational leadership and cultural studies, MSA coordinator, internship coordinator, and principal fellows coordinator at the University of North Carolina at Greensboro. She received her doctorate from the University of North Carolina at Greensboro. She has served as teacher, assistant principal, principal, and central office leader in North Carolina school systems. She is currently the principal investigator of a research project, *Investigating Sustained Staff Development on the*

Performance of Assistant Principals in Their Current Roles and as Newly Appointed Principals, focused on three areas of leadership: instructional leadership, management and operations, and school climate and culture.